The 2020 Diocesan Anniversary Edition

HOLY ORDERS HOLY WATERS

*Re-Exploring the Compelling Influence of
Charleston's Bishop John England &
Monsignor Joseph L. O'Brien*

W. THOMAS McQUEENEY

Palmetto Publishing Group
Charleston, SC

Holy Orders, Holy Waters
Copyright © 2020 by W. Thomas McQueeney

All rights reserved

First Edition

Printed in the United States

Hardcover: 978-1-64111-888-0
Paperback: 978-1-64111-883-5
eBook: 978-1-64111-212-3

CONTENTS

DEDICATION:
TO BISHOP DAVID B. THOMPSON

Bishop David B. Thompson
Photo Courtesy Diocese of Charleston.

It follows in sequence that the spiritual guidance and leadership of a diocese falls upon the episcopate designated to the task. The propitious appointment of Bishop David B. Thompson as coadjutor Bishop of Charleston in May of 1989 brought a true pastoral dialogue to the Holy City. Like Bishop John England and Monsignor Joseph Laurence O'Brien, Bishop Thompson inventoried what was there to find out what was missing. For him, the chasm was evident. The timeliness of inter-faith discourse was prioritized in an era when there were concerns of so much ambivalence in the secular world. Too many good young people were joining the legions of the un-churched. For this reason Bishop Thompson planned a conference of statewide churches and synagogues. Discussions promoted a better understanding of religious importance and diversity in communities.

Energetic and determined, Bishop Thompson visited every parish in the Diocese and returned often as his way of being personally available to all whom he could assist. His pastoral letter, "Our Heritage—Our Hope", initiated the Synod of Charleston—an official gathering of the Catholic community. The discourse was completed over nearly five years and did much to foster growth and to advance religious vocations.

It was the leadership of Bishop Thompson that the move of Bishop England High School to the Daniel Island site was orchestrated in 1998.[1] This process had begun in 1995 with the donation of forty acres from the Harry Frank Guggenheim Foundation. That construction was one of many timely Diocesan capital improvements made over the bishop's tenure.

Bishop Thompson, at 75, stepped down from his role in 1999 as he had reached the age of mandatory retirement. Yet the Diocese of Charleston was further blessed with his devoted service for another 15 years. His regular Sunday Mass at Christ Our King Parish was a treat for the worshippers. He crafted his brilliant three-point homilies to perfec-tion. He did so without notes. He cited all who assisted from the choir to the readers, Eucharistic Ministers to the alter servers—by the warmth of friendship and sincere appreciation, always by their first names. His ingenuity, academic insights, and incredible powers of recall had been among his most charming personal traits, notwithstanding his constan-cy of humility and humor.

Though Bishop Thompson received many accolades during his decade-long pastorate, he was most humbled by the unexpected honor that reached into his remarkable interfaith friendships. The *Tree of Life Award* was presented to him as a result of his constancy in the promotion of interreligious harmony. The distinction represents the highest award given by the Jewish National Fund. As the eleventh Bishop of Charleston, the meaningful presentation is most mindful of the inherent community strengths of Charleston's first bishop, John England.

Gravestone of Bishop David B. Thompson
Photo by Author.

Bishop Thompson passed away on November 24th, 2013, at the age of 90. He was interred at the left side of the Cathedral of St. John the Baptist. There, one might find a new golf ball placed above his gravestone each November 24. It was through his friendship, guidance, and insight that the production of this work was planned. It is to him, a man I deeply admired, that this work is dedicated.

W. Thomas McQueeney

FOREWORD

It is in the time of the Coronavirus COVID-19 that has devasted so many lives around the world that the Diocese of Charleston has had to adapt to what became the "new normal." Plans for celebrations were altered. The namesake high school of Bishop John England dispersed their student body in the beginning of March of 2020 with little hope that that class would attend a formal graduation ceremony. The most significant upheaval in anyone's memory occurred, as ordered by the Diocese—Easter was canceled. The danger of congregations was all-too real. People were dying—family members, neighbors, and religious leaders.

Sometimes we look around and notice that something we championed as important should be celebrated, but nobody thought to send out the invitations. This was acknowledged in 2012 when the 200th Anniversary of the War of 1812 rolled in and out of the calendar with barely a discernible yawn. Our South Carolina native son, "Old Hickory" Andrew Jackson, would be more than a bit dismayed. It was bad enough that he had engineered that war's most significant American victory, only to incur the historical footnote that his heroic victory happened two weeks after the war had ended![2]

Understanding the dynamics of the world in which we live, it seems that everyone has a full schedule of other priorities—and so much of those are the sedentary urgencies imposed by electronic media. We have emailed, tweeted, and Facebooked our way into cyber-ambivalence. The coronavirus exacerbated this nuance. People needed people, if only for a message or a photo or an emoji. It's noteworthy that prior to the coronavirus pandemic, a daily dialogue with the keyboard-menacing masses had pre-empted centuries of one-on-one conversation with facial expressions, voice inflections, and the pauses that emphasize introspective thought.

Bishop John England 1796-1842
Photo Courtesy Bishop England High School

In the burgeoning world of Charleston, South Carolina, the celebration that was in order, had been mostly ordered mute. The Diocese of Charleston had reached its 200th year. The first Catholic Bishop of Charleston, John England, first came to Charleston on the last day of 1820. The namesake high school, where students might have been unaware of the major significance of John England, had recently celebrated its one-hundredth year. Bishop John England Memorial High School, as it was officially named, also represented a major step forward for Catholicity in South Carolina. But the students were home immersed in online classes because of the worldwide pandemic, Coronavirus COVID-19. These had become unusual times.

Five years prior to this effort, as someone proud of my Catholic Faith, I decided not to let a one-hundred-year anniversary of the high school pass without homage to two Irish priests. One became the high school's namesake; the other its founder. They lived nearly a century apart but had so much in common that it inspired the effort. Bishop John England and Monsignor Joseph Laurence "Doc" O'Brien deserve the profound appreciation of a diocese that flourished by way of their toil.

Noting that the year 2020 would herald another important arrival anniversary, it was incumbent upon me that I re-focused an effort to perform what I had, regrettably, omitted in the first effort. I went to Ireland to walk the steps of the great bishop. I went to his childhood school, his parish church, his cathedral, his first pastorate, and to the seemingly impossible last parish he administered in duress. That holy adventure provided the realization that the much-researched 2014 book I had authored begged for a completer and more updated edition.

The two-hundred-year anniversary of the year that John England landed at a wharf on Charleston harbor had arrived. He came from a much larger city of Cork, Ireland. It was a repressive city with many more Catholics—but all held in a contemptuous relationship with the ruling British government. It was a hard place. It was also a hard place to leave.

An Irish Memorial was installed in Charleston in 2013 at the foot of Charlotte Street. It borders the harbor. The large granite map of Ireland is not likely to be moved by Charleston's famous engagements with disaster— natural and man-made. The Irish contributions to Catholicity in Charleston, in secular leadership roles, and in economic entrepreneurship cannot be fully appreciated. The names read as eponyms—Morrison Drive, Byrnes Down, Riley Park, Murray Boulevard. They will continue. As recently as 2019, the Bennett Hotel opened as perhaps the most opulent in the state. Michael Bennett was the major donor to The Mayor's Gate—as part of the Irish Memorial.

In summation of this updated investigation into two holy lives, consider it an apologetic oversight. I should have found more about John England on that other continent. I realized it after the first publication and made the corrective journey.

With sincere thanks to the sharing of documents and information from the Diocese of Charleston Diocesan Archivist Brian Fahey, the generous donation of artifacts from the O'Brien family, and the initial encouragement from the eleventh Bishop of Charleston, Most Reverend David B. Thompson, the following second edition pages are presented. I also benefitted from the benevolence of the administration of Bishop England High School, and the Marlene and Nathan Addlestone Library at the College of Charleston. Ironically, that library is situated upon the former site of Bishop England High School (1922-1998) and the Father O'Brien Gymnasium (1948-1998). This is the school I attended for four years from 1966 to 1970. Some would say they should have kept me longer.

I had the propitious fortune of friendship with a special Irish couple, Eamonn and Karen Cassidy. Karen, a fine research historian, supplied support information that would have bobbled in the Atlantic Ocean otherwise. It seems that ocean had swallowed much of the John England family information over two centuries 'trasna na dtonnta' (Gaelic for 'across the seas'), as Karen noted. Karen supplied much genealogical information that had scarcely been associated with the England family on the shores west of Ireland. Her husband Eamonn has spent his career in activities associated with tourism. His natural demeanor is to welcome others to the Emerald Isle.

I am grateful to Sister Anne Francis Campbell, Archivist for the Sisters of Charity of Our Lady of Mercy, for allowing me access to relevant material in the Congregation's archives, and, for sharing her knowledge of the life and times of Bishop John England and Monsignor J. L. "Doc" O'Brien. She is a brilliant and insightful steward of Catholic historical documents.

My father, who passed away in 2011, spurred my own personal interest in this subject. William T. McQueeney found his finest life's mentor, Monsignor "Doc" O'Brien. The founder of Bishop England High School became my father's compass point, not only in his faith, but also in his comportment of other areas of life.

My father was not alone. In my research I have found so many other contemporary references to this great priest, who died five days before I was born. Accompanied by my father, the very pregnant Charlotte

Simmons McQueeney attended his funeral. So, one could say, I was there, too!

Monsignor O'Brien's reach certainly remained beyond the span of his life. Indeed, in speaking with three BEHS graduates, Walter V. Duane, Helen Dodds Shepherd, and John LaTorre, I found that students were positively impacted over his long tenure as Rector of the high school. The entire student population shared the endearing moniker "Doc," ascribed to the holy man. It was a nickname he preferred. To be sure, Doc O'Brien built a lasting impression upon countless students.

Duane, from the Bishop England Class of 1939, gave first-hand testimony.

Walter V. Duane 2017
Photo by Author

"Bishop England High School sent more than our share to fight in World War II. He would send each of us personal encouragement letters every month during the war. It made you feel special that he cared. And he'd sign every one of them "Doc." It was his way of keeping you informed of the happenings in Charleston and at dear old Bishop England. If you were a Bishop England High School graduate in the military service, you got a regular post from Doc. The art of letters has diminished over the generations, as has the energy and time it takes to show personal care and concern. Monsignor O'Brien was especially adept at remaining a part of each student's life well after high school."

Walter Duane, a dear family friend, died on May 21, 2017 at the age of 95. I was wholly encouraged in my task by Walter.

Helen Dodds Shepherd stopped by my office on occasion. She graduated in the Bishop England High School Class of 1945. She remembered the Monsignor fondly for his disciplined demeanor, yet caring attitude for all students. She concurred with the Duane remarks.

"I was younger and was in the high school during the war. Father O'Brien was a true patriot and did so much to inspire and to boost the morale of those overseas fighting for freedom and our way of life," Shepherd recalled. "He was an extraordinary priest whom we all deeply admired. He was both a respected authority and a caring friend."

Sadly, Mrs. Shepherd passed away on October 22, 2017, at the age of 88. There were others, many still living.

"He changed my life," John LaTorre confided.

From the Class of 1948, LaTorre went off to college at the University of South Carolina to play football. "I confided in "Doc" that I had reached a point where I had made up my mind to drop out of college. In just a few days, I received a handwritten letter of encouragement from Doc convincing me that I needed to work hard and continue my education. That letter changed my life. I still have that letter as one of my most cherished possessions. I know he looked after a lot of people, but I always felt he took a special interest in me and that's why I can never forget this amazing priest."

In preparing this work, it became clear that Monsignor O'Brien had studied Bishop John England in both an academic and a pastoral light. The hundredth anniversary of the founding of the high school provided a reason for the study; the exuberance for the topic soon followed.

To properly celebrate this anniversary, it would be most beneficial to re-establish the significance of the name "John England." In doing so, I found a brave man who not only changed his home country, but also brought his convictions to the American South. As in Ireland, his reputation and impact grew to proportions that exceeded his 56 years on earth. I was more-than-pleasantly surprised at the regard they held for Bishop England upon my visit to Cork. He was much studied, and much admired in places well beyond his assigned three-state Diocese.

Bishop England High School began in the old Cathedral School in 1915, then moved the following year to the building where the Cenacle Sisters once lived on Calhoun Street. The redbrick enclave was completed on the adjoining lots in 1922. That school remained until 1998 when the high school was moved to a college-like campus on Daniel Island. The alumni include a most healthy share of scholars, priests and nuns, entrepreneurs, political figures, business leaders, and others dedicated to the Catholic way of life. There are several families who now boast of a fourth generation of graduates. A monsignor's vision of a co-educational parochial high school found a niche that perhaps only he saw in 1914.

A Century of Catholic Education

**The logo celebrating the high school's 100 Years.
Logo Courtesy Bishop England High School.**

There were other major impactful moments worldwide in 1914. It was the same year that Archduke Ferdinand was assassinated in Serbia, the kindling that lit World War I. The Panama Canal opened, shortening travel between the two great oceans. Owing to hostilities with Mexico, American Marines occupied Vera Cruz. George Washington

Carver, the son of a slave, began to revolutionize southern farming by virtue of his experiments with the peanut.

The year 1920—the Diocese's one-hundredth year—was still reeling from the Great War in addition to that last world pandemic, erroneously called the Spanish Flu.[3]

This effort is not so much for posterity as it is for the students and the parents of students—who may realize that they are enjoying special opportunities because of two visionaries. It is for the posterity of Catholics who enjoy the fruits of what was sewn by two visionaries. These sacrifices were made by the two clerics who lived a century apart

Topical and biographical research remains, perhaps, among the most tedious tasks necessary for every level of academia. The process of assembling the facts, the photographs, and the letters of correspondence would—for the author (me)—also develop into interviews and even the support reference of foreign travel. The travel was for research and resulted in the reflection-connection of resources. By my good fortune, I had been to Ireland ten times (by the publication of this second edition)—and to Cork City seven times. Bandon (fifteen miles to the southwest) and Carlow (closer to Dublin) conjured the early years of Bishop England for me. St. Patrick College in Carlow had been founded near the time of England's birth, and became a seminary (exclusively) for one hundred years. The college remains as an esteemed institution educating students in a spectrum of undergraduate programs and post-graduate law. Among its distinguished graduates are "other famous" Catholic clergy, Most Reverend John Therry (first Bishop of Australia), and Most Reverend Paul Cullen, the first Irish Cardinal.[4]

By good fortune, I also traveled to Switzerland six times. It is a country of wondrous alpine scenery, much as I had dreamed to experience in my early parochial school geography lessons. Fribourg, where Joseph Laurence O'Brien studied at the old university, is less than twenty miles from Bern. Like St. Patrick College in Carlow, the University of Fribourg remains a center of classical learning and academic research.

Other reference data was found. I gained new information from the archival files that the O'Brien family had kept and recently donated to the Diocese of Charleston. My friend, Tom O'Brien, handed the material to me personally! I carefully repaired old photographs digitally. Key quotes were re-discovered such as Monsignor O'Brien's own words describing the choice of Bishop John England as the namesake for the new high school. We know that choice to be quite appropriate.

For the record, I loathe the tediousness of research like mostly everyone else and I pre-apologize for the preponderance of the very necessary and voluminous footnotes. However, the more I delved into the subject, the more I found the need of the research— and the steering currents of the professionals that assisted me. As mentioned, they did so at great sacrifice of their own precious time.

Our modern world boasts of Generation X, the babies of the post World War II Baby Boomers, and their children, the Millennials. What this work purports to accomplish in its re-discovery of meaningful diocesan history and the accompanying biographical insights is to explain the foundational sense of the past before we encounter a "Generation Who." They will, no doubt, find much more to every answer than my generation, as Baby Boomers, could have ever fathomed. My generation diligently searched to find small bits of dated information by the Dewey Decimal System and the bleary-eyed reading of pertinent materials. The generation that reads this minor work will likely enjoy a deluge of information readily. Technologies will take them further than my imagination can comprehend.

We owe much to two gentlemen who lived a century apart. One was a newly consecrated Irish Bishop for the recently created Diocese of Charleston, crossing the Atlantic to a new world of promise. Another was an Irish American scholar from Pennsylvania who had earnestly studied the life of that same bishop before arriving in Charleston. Our "Holy City" waterfront welcomed both.

They have truly established the natural harbor we enjoy as holy waters.

CHAPTER ONE

LIKE STATIONS OF THE CROSS

We should stop and reflect. It should be a law of personal life choices. We should look past facts to determine what they mean to humanity, to a culture, or to an individual. We should internalize meaning. After all, what is life if we become robotic, if we do not live purposefully? There should always be a passion within a pursuit.

The Stations of the Cross were derived from an actual path. The Via Dolorosa in Jerusalem is the holy path taken by Jesus as he painfully trudged the way to his crucifixion at Mt. Calvary.[5] It was the path that changed mankind forever.

There are fourteen Stations of the Cross (as there are fourteen chapters herein). Reflection gives meaning. Imagine that it is your last day on earth much as Christ knew. Imagine the insults, the exhaustion, the pain, the cruelty, and the forgiveness. What does it mean? Stop at each station and think about the action and the inclination.

"Jesus is Condemned to Death. Jesus Falls for the First Time. Veronica Wipes the Face of Jesus. Jesus is Crucified. Jesus is Laid in the Tomb." The experience is compelling to each of us two thousand years later. They have moved the world. Contemplation is observed at each station.

The retrieval of information needed to fully appreciate the lives of two clergymen who lived a century apart brought new insights. As we sometimes do—we accept the facts, the dates, and the events without the connecting tissue that makes each relevant. As an example, we may read factually that a young priest traveled from the Scranton area of Pennsylvania in 1914 to work in the rather depressive southern city of Charleston (as it surely was at that time). Charleston had suffered a recent series of tragedies that included a substantial earthquake (1886), two major hurricanes (1891 and 1913), and an economic calamity that lasted nearly one hundred years after the Civil War. There were hundreds of Confederate Veterans living in Charleston along with their progeny. They harbored a willful discontent.

To illustrate the vitriol passed to future generations, it was not unusual to hear the words *damn* and *Yankee* as if it were a singular term in the 1960s. I know this because my grandmother (1900-1982) held a discernible bias. She was not unlike the rest of the Charleston population. Yet, a Yankee priest came here with plans to begin a Catholic education system beyond the parochial level. He could not have been initially endeared. By the time Monsignor Joseph Laurence O'Brien passed away in Charleston on March 3, 1952, he was among the most beloved clerics in the history of the Diocese of Charleston. Surely, he was subjected to early scorn and disdain. He handled it quite well. I have a younger brother named for this great man.

Imagine coming to the most active North American port of the detestable slave trade in 1820. Arriving from a country of similar repression—his beloved Ireland—he was an outspoken critic of the horrid institution. Yet, in time he was also welcomed by the population as a fine academic and a pious holy man. His views may have been held in contempt by many, but his impact upon both the secular and religious communities was historically dynamic.

The contemplation of the travails these two Catholic gentlemen incurred in adverse climates may assist one in the inspection of their accomplishment. It could be determined that their arrivals were met with much controversy—and in the case of John England—vitriol. Neither of these gentlemen had become initially embraced. They each enhanced their eventual admiration from the tepid cauldron of adverse beginnings. It would take much fortitude to stay the course.

Bishop John England and Monsignor Joseph Laurence O'Brien rose to become significant and consequential characters in the religious development of Charleston and the State of South Carolina. There are contemplative achievements beyond.

The low profile of Charleston in 1820 remains in Charleston of 2020.
Photo courtesy of Charleston Museum.

Chapter Two

BRETHREN OF RISK

Bishop John England and his biographer, Monsignor Joseph Laurence 'Doc' O'Brien, were risk-takers who shared much more than their Irish heritage. They changed not only Catholicity in Charleston, but also furthered the acceptance of the previously downtrodden Catholics statewide.

All religions were guaranteed freedoms by the John Locke "Fundamental Constitutions of Carolina."[6] Well, almost. That constitution was never ratified by the governing assembly but did have the shadow of religious freedom—inviting Jews, Lutherans, Quakers and others to the new beginnings.[7] Owing to European conflict, Catholics were not welcome. Though the American Revolution expanded freedoms, that expansion was not extended to all citizens. They were still uneasy about Catholics because they represented warring countries of France and Spain. All of Catholic Ireland had been repressed for centuries. Others not embraced were those that came to America—not of their own volition. Slavery existed. And despite the intent of the document, the shadow of religious bias existed, as well.

The new times of Catholic enterprise brought just the right man to the southern harbor that the sea currents washed into destiny – Charleston. The early twentieth century produced another priest to be a catalyst of faith-building in the harbor of learning. They were somewhat the same cleric, only separated by a century. Their one kindred calling uplifted many a searching soul, regardless of religious affiliation. They each left the known comforts of their respective families.

Risk was a given in most ways of American life in the times of these two priests. There was the robust risk of sickness—cholera, malaria, tuberculosis, and yellow fever were ever present in both centuries. Neither priest had the early advantage of vaccinations that had changed life expectancy—from Alexander Fleming's penicillin (1928) for infectious disease to Dr. Jonas Salk's polio prevention (1953).[8] Other risk was evident by the stream of constant human conflict – wars and political upheavals that ravaged generations of youth across the world. Both England and O'Brien had known the disasters (the ongoing Irish struggles and penal codes of the early 19th century and America's Great Depression in the 1930's). Charleston was built for risk, owing to the devastation expected from the great storms that marched across the mid-Atlantic Ocean each year. A hurricane was never a surprise to a Charlestonian.

A citizen of Charleston would expect risk as much as one would expect justice, commerce, and societal interaction. But all were treated in the heartbeat of life—with varying degrees of impact. When Bishop England arrived, the societal risks were evident –an economy based on slavery and religious toleration evident in theory, but not in practice. When Father O'Brien came from Pennsylvania, he was met with a strong southern predisposition of distrust of 'Yankee' oversight partially from veterans of the Confederate States of America scattered about Charleston in 1914. His arrival was nearly fifty years after the cessation of North-South hostilities. He anticipated the adversity.

Risk begets reward, especially when the diligence of purpose is cemented.

Both Bishop England and Monsignor O'Brien left a legacy of that dedication, showing an industrious and energetic spirit with an overcrowded résumé for a singular lifetime. They lived wide. The summary of their individual accomplishment had filled pages. The citations of greatness were not what they had each intended. They took risks to gain the value of significance. They each donated their expertise, their energy, and their existence to causes greater than themselves. They benefitted innumerable others in the form of leadership, learning, and lasting institutions. They bolstered faith. Their separate legacies remain as exemplary lives based within selfless aspects.

By example, the young priest John England, of Cork, found the inequities of living under British rule a matter to be rectified. His intellect, oratory, and writing skills tested those that governed to extreme limits. Two centuries later, those scholars who lauded his bold efforts to bring social justice to the Irish assert his life was in danger. Leaving Ireland likely saved him from a dreaded fate.

It is in the spirit of discovery and re-discovery of what two gentlemen priests have borne and bequeathed that underscores their tolerance of risk in a world riddled with its debris. Fear of failure could be its own catalyst. It is certainly a better condition than the more available reason—fear of effort.

Marian statue near Margaret and Dunbar Street in Cork City, Ireland.
Photo by author.

CHAPTER THREE

CATHOLIC BEGINNINGS IN THE AMERICAN SOUTH

In order to bring the young Bishop, John England, to the new three-state Diocese of Charleston, it would be useful to set the existing state of Catholicism in the American South, and especially in Charleston. By the bishop's own calculations, there were only seven thousand five hundred Catholics in all of South Carolina – and less in the adjoining states. Only five hundred lived in North Carolina and about three thousand in Georgia.[9] The European nationalities that had delivered this Catholic population were mostly French and Irish. Both were newly arrived, owing to incidents elsewhere. The French came from two specific events, an uprising in Santo Domingo (known historically as the 1791 Haitian Revolution).[10] The other French Catholic faction arrived sporadically from the aftermath and chaos of the French Revolution (1789).[11] The Irish that came were from yet another attempted revolution, set in 1798, and modeled after the American Revolution of 1776.[12] It's short duration and failure made an escape from Ireland necessary for Catholics that were part of the Society of United Irishmen.[13] The new United States of America had the promise of religious freedom that gave each group a new start in a country of much promise. After all, they had stood down the most powerful country on earth, the British.

It is historically evident that John Locke's *Fundamental Constitutions of Carolina* provided the impetus of religious freedom and was a major source work for the United States Constitution. Jews, Quakers, and the French Huguenots came to Charles Towne (renamed to 'Charleston' after the Revolution). Catholics were in another category. Restrictive British law had previously prevented parishes in the Carolinas. Why? There was a societal attitude that "from the sixteenth century, Englishmen pictured the Roman Church not merely as a system of cruelty and intolerance, but as an international conspiracy operating through secret agents and with the covert sympathy of fellow travellers."[14] These awkward beliefs from the Protestant-dominated society of young America prevailed in the mindset of the new nation—even though the rights of man, tolerance, and freedom were being championed. Indeed, after the Revolution, religious acceptance often drifted to old world divides—gaps betraying the intention of the U.S. Constitution's First Amendment.

As a British colony, the dominant churches were the Church of England (Episcopal) and the Church of Scotland (Presbyterian). The emancipation from British rule with the Treaty of Paris (1783) meant that the French and Irish were no longer coming to a British world, but rather to a world of unbridled freedoms. Nonetheless, Catholics remained in a lower level of citizenship due to the extant and lingering British customs. In many quarters, "the Papists" were despised by association to factions in almost every old-world connotation—with the warring Spanish, the aristocratic French, as well as the subjugated Irish Catholics. Those anti-Catholic attitudes may still exist today in some pockets of Americana.

St. Mary of the Annunciation Catholic Church.
Photo by author.

By history's acknowledgement, the French Catholics were in need of a congregational assembly. They rented, then purchased a house and lot on Hasell Street (1788) and formed the Church of St. Mary of the Annunciation (August, 1789).[15] The Irish Catholics were part of their early membership, and became robust in their parish growth. The French incorporated the conformity they practiced in the West Indies to appoint a council of church oversight—a vestry. This system mirrored practices of the Episcopal faith in Charleston at that time.

The first three priests of the St. Mary's congregation were Irish—Father Matthew Ryan, Father Thomas Keating, and Father Simon Felix Gallagher. Through expectations of traditional Vatican allegiance, the lay trustees of St. Mary's – the vestry – struggled with the friction of pastoral authority. The early abiding authority remained with the vestry. Later, "at a vestry meeting on March 26th, 1810 a resolution was passed to appoint a committee to draw up new rules for the future government of the church."[16] That resolution denied the vote or presence of the pastor at vestry meetings. This was a puzzling and non-conforming disconnect! The powerful lay vestry had excluded the parish priest. That vestry was comprised of a cross section of parishioners, though most, by 1810, were of Irish birth or Irish decent.[17]

Archbishop Ambrose Marèchal of Baltimore 1817-1828.
Photo Courtesy Diocese of Baltimore.

By 1816, it became apparent that the vestry of St. Mary's and the Archbishop of Baltimore, who had full oversight, were to remain at odds. Concurrently, in Ireland, the events that led to Father England's elevation were in progress. The contemporaneous timing was, in fact, related.

> *"In 1817, Father England resigned his trusteeship with the Chronicle and accepted a pastorship of the church of Bandon, a town about sixteen miles southwest of Cork City. While the young pastor was devoting himself to his new duties, schism was racking the Church in faraway Charleston, South Carolina. As the particulars involve a long and complicated story, suffice it to say that lay trusteeism and rampant nationalism had combined to produce the scandalous situation. Put simply, the schism occurred in 1816 when the lay trustees of*

Saint Mary's, the only Catholic congregation in Charleston, refused to accept as their pastor the French-born Father J.P. DeCloriviere appointed by the Archbishop of Baltimore. The Archbishop placed Saint Mary's under interdict. Father DeCloriviere then opened a chapel on Cannon Street and Ashley Avenue for the members of the congregation willing to submit to the Archbishop's authority. Matters came to a head in 1819 when the schismatics promoted a scheme to establish an Independent Catholic Church with an Irish priest consecrated by the Jansenist Bishop of Utrecht as its head. The Archbishop of Baltimore, the Most Reverend Ambrose Marechal dispatched Father Benedict Fenwick, S.J., the future Bishop of Boston, to Charleston to remove the interdict as soon as the trustees would submit to authority. Father Fenwick managed to restore some semblance of peace and unity, yet the attempt to form an Independent Church convinced Rome that something had to be done. Acting upon Archbishop Marechal's suggestion, the Sacred Congregation of Propaganda decided to detach the Carolinas and Georgia from the Archdiocese of Baltimore and form them into a new Diocese with the Bishop's residence in Charleston. In June, 1820, having studied the problem for a year, the Sacred Congregation recommended and Pope Pius VII approved the erection of the See of Charleston with John England as its first Bishop."[18]

The trustee system became a common practice in the new United States, since religious entities were not allowed to own property. Monsignor Joseph Laurence O'Brien's 1934 publication, *John England: The Apostle to Democracy*, explains this dynamic.

"American Catholic Church history has been marred much more by the specter than the reality of Trusteeism, which ever since has been used by the bishops as a club to keep the laity

in submission. The laws of the new nation required that church property be placed in the possession of a lay corporation; in the early American Catholic churches this corporation was known as the trustees, and it operated much as was already the case in French Canada at that time. For the great majority of cases this system worked very well, but in a small minority of cases, partly because of manipulative Irish priests and partly because of some poor administrative tactics by several bishops, cases of serious open conflict between the bishop and the trustees of certain churches developed – in one case a young lawyer named Abraham Lincoln defended the trustees. Because of their notoriety these few cases attained more importance than they intrinsically merited, and the fumbling of the bishops only tended to exacerbate the problems.

Charleston of 1820 was the scene of one of the longest and most bitter of these trustee conflicts. One might have expected that the situation might have forced a vigorous young bishop from outside the United States to make authoritative kinds of moves. Nothing, however, could have been farther from the truth with Bishop John England. His initial and subsequent actions were the very epitome of toleration, democracy and voluntarism. For England, the evils of Trusteeism were the result of the failure of proper constitutional provisions in the original trustee charters. England responded to the sources of these evils by creating his constitutional form of government."[19]

In the few years leading up to the establishment of the Charleston Diocese, the first Archdiocese of the United States was established in Baltimore. John Carroll (1735-1815) was consecrated as the first United States Archbishop. Archbishop Carroll was the cousin of Charles Carroll of Carrollton—the only Catholic to sign the Declaration of

Independence.[20] After Archbishop Carroll's passing, his successor, Archbishop Leonard Neale had an abbreviated tenure, dying in 1817. The French immigrant Archbishop Ambrose Maréchal followed.

The multi-talented and controversial Father Limoëlan de Clorivière.
Photo courtesy Gibbes Art Gallery, Charleston.

Joseph-Pierre Picot de Limoëlan de Clorivière (1768-1826)[21], the priest that had to move to Cannon Street, would warrant a full study separate of this work. The priest that St. Mary's parish would not initially accept had an interesting pre-ordination résumé. He was an adventurer, a successful businessman, an accomplished artist, and was the only man to escape an assassination attempt on Napoleon's life! Some of his miniature portraits are presently displayed in Charleston's Gibbes Art Gallery.

Another person of historic interest emerged from the transitional times to the authority of John England. Father Simon Felix Gallagher, the second pastor of St. Marys, was one of the eight founders of the Hibernian Society of Charleston (formed 1799, chartered 1801). He became the first president of that society, the oldest benevolent Irish society in America.

It was because of the efforts of the Jesuit Father Benedict Fenwick that Bishop England could begin his 1820s tenure in Charleston without the impediments of St. Mary's lay vestry. Within thirteen months, the issue had been resolved and this landmark church and assembly graduated to the affairs of traditional canon law.

It was Father Fenwick who met the ship that brought Bishop John England from Ireland. The new bishop was quickly apprised of all matters and began his duties in humble service to all that he had inherited in the three-state diocese.

> "Bishop England's first response to the challenge of schism was both peaceful and wise. Giving not the least hint of anger or revenge, he took no legal action and imposed no church penalties on the troublemakers.... He quietly negotiated a three-year lease of St. Mary's Church from the trustees, rather than making himself their hostage by using a church they controlled. At the same time, he arranged for the construction of another church, which could be designated as Charleston's Cathedral. He did what he had been ordained to do: he watched over and ministered to the people as their priest. Before long, the great majority of Charleston's Catholic community found themselves touched by the openness and kindness of their new bishop. They recognized in him a true spiritual shepherd, and they followed his lead. The trustees, for the most part, were left talking to themselves. (Father) Gallagher departed for Florida with England's blessing. Arranging a full reconciliation with the stubborn trustees would take more time and considerable patience on the part of the new bishop. It was already clear, however, that he had won the contest in Charleston. And he had done it as a man of peace."[22]

In his diary that he kept since 1821, Bishop England expressed the concern of losing good Catholic parishioners over the politics of church authority. His concern was that they would become Methodists, who were aggressive in their recruitment at the time.[23]

The bishop had broader activities to attend. Catholics in a three-state diocese needed the full benefit of the Sacraments. It was important to travel to the remote regions and to celebrate Mass within the myriad sheltered venues that were not Catholic churches.

Charleston was once a walled city—the only British walled city in North America. The walls came down in due course, once the British ruled the seas. The city itself became among the most affluential in the Western Hemisphere. By 1790, it boasted the fourth largest population in the former colonies, only trailing New York, Philadelphia and Boston.[24] By Bishop England's arrival, it was sixth, surpassed by Baltimore and New Orleans (not a U.S. city in 1790).[25] There was wealth. There was optimism. There was growth. John England had arrived at a place where the exuberance of a burgeoning America was still evident, but where the Catholic Church was mired into the status of a mission effort. He recognized the work to be done.

One could postulate, that given the foundation of religious freedom and the exposure to world trade, Charleston was destined to become a fine port welcoming all faiths. But that was not the case upon England's arrival. It took the right man at the correct time. Fate played remarkable music in the small ensemble of Catholic beginnings in the Holy City.

St. Mary's Church became an important bastion of Catholicity in the Carolinas for the next two hundred years. The second Charleston church, St. Finbar's – built near Broad and Legare Streets – initiated another foundation of worshippers. St. Finbar's possessed the added advantage of a man considered among the greatest orators of his time, Bishop John England.

The Cathedral of St. John the Baptist, Charleston.
Photo by author.

Part of St. Finbar's eventual reconstruction as the Cathedral of St. John the Baptist houses the vault that is graced with John England's remains. Symbolically, the Cathedral was built upon John England's work. In a larger sense, Catholicism in the Carolinas and Georgia would point to this man as that spiritual foundation.

CHAPTER FOUR

ENGLAND'S IRELAND

B ishop John England accompanied by his sister, Joanna, and Father Denis Corkery arrived in Charleston from Ireland on December 30th of 1820. He traveled to Charleston aboard the ship *Thomas Gelston*.[26] He championed the American way of life in his oratory. Freedom mattered. In Ireland, there was no such fulfillment for Catholics under the stringency of British rule.

Timing was favorable for the young John England. Through a full century of excruciating Penal Codes, the Irish had precious few rights. A timely repeal of some of the codes (from 1778 to 1793) advanced John England's opportunities. It was not until 1778 that the codes even allowed a Catholic to marry a Protestant. By that same year, a ban on some the codes allowed the Irish to lease land. Though the difficulties were lessening in the late eighteenth century, the British-Irish conflicts continued into recent times.[27]

England was born in 1786, the first of ten children.[28] His natural thirst for knowledge propelled him. His family had weathered the failed Irish Rebellion of 1798 when John was only 14. They were certainly familiar with the strife of the era.

> *"John England's family had suffered under the tyranny of the anti-Catholic Penal Codes. His grandfather had been imprisoned for four years, and his father, threatened with transportation to the West Indies for the terrible crime of teaching*

school, had spent a year hiding in the mountains of County Cork."[29]

One early penal law disallowed an Irishman to gain an education at a Protestant school (repealed by law of 1782). England was able to attend the Green Coat School, this being previously an all-Protestant institution for young boys. This was the first of several ameliorations of Irish law that had great benefit to his generation.

Gates of the Green Coat School, Cork.
Photo by Eamonn Cassidy.

With intentions to enter the legal profession, England spent two years studying law, also recently allowed by a repeal. His later diary speaks to these times and his decision to enter the Seminary of St. Patrick at Carlow. He was only 17. He was torn between the need for Irish political leadership and the dedication of his life to religious orders. As his life evolved, he was able to perform both functions simultaneously.

England had studied the model of American democracy and had adopted America in his mind and heart well before he crossed the Atlantic. He considered the words, "inalienable rights," that changed the world from classist ideology to the rights of every man. The American Declaration of Independence was, to him, the embodiment of timely secular freedoms established as a model for the world. He printed words of the first amendment of the United States Constitution as a banner above his later landmark American publication, *The United States Catholic Miscellany*:

> "*Congress shall make no law respecting an establishment of religion, or prohibiting the free exercise thereof.*"

England saw the expressions of freedom as something that could flourish in the mind of like-minded people. But he had the old world contentiousness to confront in Ireland. His constant editorial challenge to the British restrictions, in view of ever-present retribution, made him a passionate leader in the eyes of his readership. England had gained a similar following for his oratory. He became a vehement advocate for change to improve the Irish condition.

> "*The young man had a great way with his pen, and his oratory, mixing a tradesman's common sense with romantic, dramatic images worthy of a poet, moved audiences, Protestant and Catholic alike, at least to sympathy if not to a singleness of opinion. He was a patriot through and through, republican in politics and Gallican in religion.*"[30]

His ordination to the priesthood on October 11th, 1808, formalized his commitment to service to Christ and the Catholic Church. In Cork, he was instrumental in the administration of several local charitable and educational institutions. He attended to an asylum, to the Cork jail, and to the soldiers at the Cork garrison.[31] By 1812 he began teaching theology at the College of St. Mary. By 1814, England published a monthly newsletter, *The Religious Repository*, and helped guide the larger 'Cork Mercantile Chronicle' to a wider readership, being its featured columnist.[32] His influence grew.

An attestation of his effectiveness as both a Catholic Priest and an important Irish leader of his generation developed from his assignment to the Bandon Church, near Cork. The famed gates of Bandon contained the warning "Turk, Jew or Atheist may enter here, but not a Papist."[33] He was not welcome. In spite of the decided bigotry and abhorrent warning, the young priest's oratorical skills soon won over many of the townsmen – of every political and religious persuasion. He became accepted in a most difficult setting – Bandon. No previous Catholic priest had attempted or achieved prominence there.

Bandon was developed as a walled town more than a century earlier and had been chartered as a Protestant-only community. Given the times, the infamous main gate still stood upon John England's arrival. Yet, even the Bandon community embraced Father England. England had proven to be a student of democracy and non-violent disagreement. He came to be admired for his elocution of pertinent socio-political matters.[34]

Even with his considerable skills, Father John England could never appease the ruling British. Timely orders soon came from Rome in June of 1820. Archbishop Ambrose Marèchal, by way of pastoral need in the fledgling United States, had created the Diocese of Charleston. Pope Pius VII appointed Father England to be become the first Bishop to serve the newly formed Diocese. Upon this elevation and ordination, the new bishop refused the customary allegiance to the British Crown, only reserving allegiance to the papacy in Rome. This egregious omission was met with rancor from the Protestant authorities whom heretofore had demanded allegiance to the British Crown for each ordained bishop. He noted to the informed authorities that he would make proper allegiance to his newly chosen country, America, and left in a matter of months for Charleston. The new diocese encompassed the states of North and South Carolina, as well as Georgia. His departure certainly diffused much more than religious and political fervor he would have supported by remaining in Ireland. It also separated him from his most vehement ally, the Irish patriot Daniel O'Connell.

England left for Charleston just six years beyond the signing of the Treaty of Ghent (1814), the official cessation of the second war of American Independence fought against the British. The Irish had their own tussle with the British, dating back centuries. And the British had no affinity for the newly ordained Bishop John England, once described as an irritant to the Crown "only exceeded by the Irish Liberator, Daniel O'Connell."[35] But O'Connell remained.

Indeed, Daniel O'Connell and John England had much in common. Both were contemporaneous graduates of St. Patrick College in Carlow, Ireland. They had become like-thinking friends. Both were outspoken leaders extolling the determination of an independent Catholic Ireland. Both believed in non-violent means to reach accord. Both were celebrated orators, well known for their ability to humor and inspire. Both died away from their beloved Ireland – O'Connell on the way to Rome at Genoa, and England in Charleston.[36] Daniel O'Connell certainly missed the wit and pen of John England. The Irish patriot lives on. In Ireland's capitol of Dublin, he is quite evident. The main thoroughfare, as well as the major bridge across the River Liffey, are both named for O'Connell. Along the route, one would find an enormous statue of the same rebellious associate of Father England – Mr. Daniel O'Connell. The two, England and O'Connell, were giants of the Irish cause and are forever linked to their times.

Statue of Irish Liberator, Daniel O'Connell, on O'Connell Street, Dublin.
Photo by Author.

Those in Charleston had no idea of the strength of character England had postured against the ruling British in Cork. Much of what came forward as his early homeland contributions to the cause of Irish independence arrived as information well after England's death, since England was loath to extoll the merits of his past. His experiences in Ireland, undisputedly, gave noble argument to injustices he encountered in America, most notably in the condition of black slavery. He had experienced the injustices of one society enforcing a will upon another in Ireland. This would give him a mindset for seeking solutions and repair in America.

He left for America quite aware of the inconsistencies but encouraged by the greatest civil promise of its age – the Constitution of the United States.

As England brought a younger sister, Joanna, with him to Charleston, the other eight siblings remained in Ireland. His brother Thomas and sister Mary (as Sister Catherine) devoted their lives to religious orders. Two of John England's nephews remained and led impactful lives in Ireland. They were also named for their uncles – John England, Professor of Physics and Natural Philosophy at Queens College (now known as University College Cork), and the young Thomas England who became the parish priest at Killavullen in North Cork.[37] At Killavullen Church there remains a monument to Father Thomas England inscribed as follows:

> *"But land or deck on*
> *You may safely reckon,*
> *Whatsoever country*
> *You come hither from,*
> *On an invitation*
> *To a jollification*
> *With a parish priest*
> *That's called 'Father Tom'"*

The England family in Ireland and abroad rose from the status of noteworthy to the level of "most significant." The bishop was an exemplary family leader who represented a quite exemplary family. The England legacy remains in the home country of Ireland, those in Cork well aware of this extraordinary prelate and the benefit that Ireland continued to receive from his relatives that remained.

A journey to Cork to explore those details is reserved for the last chapter of this production.

John England's Ireland and his America were both beset by prejudices. There were great divides. The eloquence he exhibited as a young priest in both written word and oratory in his native Ireland set a fine foundation for his impassioned following in America.

CHAPTER FIVE

UPON THE PIER OF THE HOLY CITY

Decembers are sometimes balmy in Charleston – a weather condition not likely in wintertime Cork. Like the weather patterns, John England hoped to find the temperature of his new home warmed by optimism and welcome. Rev. Benedict Fenwick, SJ, met England at the pier on the last Sunday of 1820. Indeed, it was the last day of 1820, the 31st.

Bishop England's new responsibility had many challenges in the new diocese. To be sure, he came from a Catholic country controlled by Protestants. The young bishop, only 34, arrived at a Protestant country slightly more tolerant of Catholics, but still not to the point of equality. The secular freedoms, Bishop England must have concluded, were well worth the new experiment of democracy. He had been challenged and had done much in the quest to improve Ireland's plight. Charleston was a new beginning.

What he accomplished as Charleston's bishop was extraordinary. It was from his enlightenment, his conviction, and his exuberance for his new country that he achieved so very much past the stretch of two decades.

> "Bishop John England had many priorities when he arrived
> in Charleston in 1820. He founded a Catholic newspaper,
> The United States Catholic Miscellany; he established the

cathedral church, St. Finbar; he opened the Seminary of St. John the Baptist to train native clergy; he dispatched what priests he had to minister to the surrounding plantations; and he founded an order of women religious, the Sisters of Charity of Our Lady of Mercy."[38]

Bishop England became a very busy leader administering a foundation of institutions needed to find Catholics, two centuries hence, established and comfortable in the profession of faith. It was not always so!

The new Bishop arrived to face newer and different prejudices than he left in Cork. No bias could have exceeded the centuries-long British disdain for Catholicism and the Irish, in general. Through those penal codes, famines, and other atrocities, the Irish were beaten down. Many had left. Indeed, in the decade between 1845 and 1855, 1.8 million Irish left the home country for other lands.[39] To stay was to face deprivation.

Bishop England, as the exceptional orator, developed a following that grew once he had arrived in Charleston. Many who enjoyed his abilities and insights were not Catholic. The respect he had gained certainly arrested much early nineteenth century anti-Catholic fervor. His travels underscored his resolve and ability to relate to the common man.

"England liked to exploit the apparent contradiction between his ecclesiastic rank and his advocacy of republican equality. On one of his many diocesan tours through Georgia and both Carolinas, he visited the remote village of Columbus, which was separated from Savannah by three hundred miles of dusty, sweaty travel in a horse-drawn jingle. As few Catholics of substance lived in the town, England had made reservations at what passed as a hotel. The townsfolk, all Protestant, eagerly crowded the lobby and waited for the strange creature to arrive. Finally, someone – surely not a Catholic bishop?— a middle-sized man, covered in road dust and sun-burnt, drew his two spent horses to a stop outside the hotel. He jumped down, strode into the lobby, 'stripped off his coat, hat, and

*vest; washed his face and hands,' and demanded a good glass
of wine, which he drank down heartily. The crowd studied his
every gesture. Only when the glass was dry did he produce
a 'large and lustrous' ring from his pocket, and, 'with his
jeweled hand,' sign his name to the register, +John Bishop of
Charleston. No doubt he meant to astonish the crowd, which
was duly astonished."[40]*

He took risks others would not dare, based on the words in that constitution he had studied in Ireland. One risk was to assist the needs of
those brought from the African continent as slaves.

*"Combating hostility to the faith, winning converts, and min-
istering to his small flock of black and white Catholics thor-
oughly occupied Bishop England. In the summer of 1835 he
opened a school for free blacks in Charleston. Taught by two
seminarians and two nuns, the school enrolled eighty students
within a few weeks. Pro slavery Charlestonians, however,
vehemently opposed the opening of this landmark school.
England saw the situation as a threat to Catholics as well as
to blacks. After a two-day standoff, he reluctantly agreed to
close the school on condition that all religious schools for free
blacks close as well as his Catholic school."[41]*

Bishop England reopened the school in 1841.

He had left a country that facilitated an authoritative society impos-
ing unjust rule upon one that was subordinated, though conditions were
not as oppressive as the practice of slavery. Nonetheless, human rights
were at risk for a class of people in Ireland. These same rights were
trampled upon in young America. He predicted its resolution.

*"Slavery, it is true, continues amongst us, and whatever may
be the opinions and desires of the South upon the subject, it
is impossible that it should be abolished for a considerable*

*time to come without the most injurious results, not merely
to property, but to society."*[42]

England's intellectual discourse was ahead of its time and much
ahead of the vehement results the South would suffer within three decades of his prophecy.

> *"A striking phase of Bishop England's apostolic character was
> manifested in his spiritual care of the negroes. He celebrated
> an early Mass in the Cathedral for them every Sunday and
> preached to them at this Mass and at a Vesper service. He
> was accustomed to deliver two afternoon sermons; if unable
> to deliver both, he would disappoint the rich and cultured
> who flocked to hear him, and preach to the poor ignorant
> Africans."*[43]

His dedication to the needs of others precluded his own. He was an
exemplary attestation to the Christ-like ideals often seen in the lives of
past Catholic Saints. He had no pretensions other than to lead by word,
action, and prayerful sacrifice.

> *"In the epidemics of those days he exhibited great devotion to
> the sick, while his priests and the Sisters of Mercy volunteered
> their services in the visitations of cholera and yellow fever.
> His personal poverty was pitiable. He was known to have
> walked the streets of Charleston with the bare soles of his feet
> to the ground. Several times the excessive fatigue and expo-
> sure incurred in his visitations and ministrations prostrated
> him, and more than once he was in danger of death. Twice
> he visited Haiti as Apostolic Delegate. In 1823 he was asked
> to take charge of East Florida and, having been given the
> powers of vicar-general, made a visitation of that territory."*[44]

Few public persons in South Carolina history to that time had attempted to do more for blacks at the risk of their own personal wellbeing than John England. To the citizenry of the 1820's – from the plantation owners to the peninsula merchants – the Catholic religion was hardly accepted. Yet the bishop's bravery, brilliance, and oratorical insights transcended much of the early divide. It was not just his conviction, but also his personality that attracted the non-Catholics to his admiration.

The new Bishop would have an opportunity to attain an admirable degree of success in Charleston with its smaller contingent of Catholics. He would perform with a fine mind of organizational methodology. Bishop England decided that to manage and administer, he would need to create a constitution for the new diocese. This action stabilized the three-state institution by giving authoritative rule and written reference to its functions.

In 1822, Bishop England had started the new St. Finbar's parish just blocks away on Broad Street, to be operated under the new Diocesan constitution he had written. Growth began in this small wooden edifice and would spread throughout the three states. The cessation of the vestry control at St. Mary's, also in 1822, galvanized the Catholic faith to move forward, beyond internal conflict. Bishop John England had become the singular authority to all Catholics in the diocese, now mended and united.

St. Mary's had a new church built in 1839 after a citywide conflagration of 1838 had destroyed the previous structure. It was Bishop John England who oversaw the replacement church. That handsome church exists today in the heightened grace and elegance exhibited in its caring reconstruction. Its architecture exudes in the warmth of faith.

The broad scope of Bishop England's energy and focus include his significant travels, yet it was upon the streets of Charleston where his reputation grew. In Charleston, the bishop preached twice on Sundays. He quickly became a popular speaker at secular functions, owing to his worldly sensibilities and brilliant delivery.

By 1822. Bishop England organized a Charleston Book Society and later that year, established the *United States Catholic Miscellany*, the first

Catholic periodical published in the United States. It continued to be published until 1861, predating the *Southern Literary Messenger* by more than a decade.[45]

The outspoken bishop opposed nullification (Nullification Act of 1832)[46] in a city where it was highly advocated. England became an active member of the Philosophical Society of Charleston, as well as organizing an Anti-dueling Society.

Bishop England was quite dismayed by an anti-Catholic oration made by Secretary of State John Quincy Adams on July 4th, 1821. It became the catalyst cause of what historians consider his most important and famous speech. He made the trip to Washington to rebut Adams, who had been elected as President of the United States.

The *National Catholic Register* properly presents this event that set the record straight about the Catholic view of church and state.

Sixth US President John Quincy Adams
Photo Courtesy Library of Congress

As what would be considered a fact-based and bold oration, Bishop John England defended the faith in front of President John Quincy Adams and others who had been previously dissuaded by Adams of the value of Catholic citizenship. This explanation of Catholicism and the benefit to America was delivered in the U.S. House of Representatives, and it marked the first time that a Catholic Bishop was invited to speak in that chamber.

> *"What is most important to us today is that Bishop England delivered a memorable speech that boldly proclaimed the beliefs of his faith while at the same time stressing its compatibility with republican virtues…The speech he delivered in Washington January 8, 1826, partly responded to anti-Catholic remarks made by John Quincy Adams in a Fourth of July oration nearly five years earlier. Adams was on hand to hear the bishop's rebuttal…In a preface to the published version of his speech, England said he had sought to address the misunderstanding that even educated people had about the beliefs of the Catholic Church. At several points in the sermon, he discussed the myths that were conveyed regarding Catholic practices, and he most certainly believed Adams was one of those mythmakers. In an age where republicanism — a commitment to equality and virtue — was strongly followed, Bishop England sought to show that Catholicism was perfectly compatible with that ideal. He also endorsed a division between religion and civil government, saying that such a dichotomy was in the best interest of both institutions. One of the bishop's biographers, Peter Clarke, has written, 'John England was the first theoretician of separation of Church and state and freedom of religion.'*

In the considerable biographical works that have inspected the life of John England, one of the thematic attributes emerges relating him as being a 'great apologist.' England was well aware of the interpretations – and misinterpretations – of the Catholic religion in the centuries leading up to the Reformation and since.

"In dissecting this notable speech, the reader is impressed by the steady, but forceful apologia offered by the Irishman. He tells the assembly, which surely was overwhelmingly non-Catholic, that the revelation of truth from the Lord was given to early Church leaders. In the first century these holy men 'formed but one Church through many nations — one tribunal to testify in every place the same doctrine — all the individuals who taught, were witnesses for or against each other: the whole body, with the successor of Peter at its head, watchful to see that each taught that which was originally delivered,' he said.

"There has been a constancy to this truth throughout the ages, and it must be presented to each age 'neither adding, omitting, [nor] changing.' After arguing the static universality of revealed truth, Bishop England then addresses the political issues that were of interest to his republican audience."[47]

In the two-hour sermon, the Bishop broaches the central subject of John Quincy Adams' earlier argument. There was much to consider in the choice of his delivery and verse as Adams, now President of the United States, stood in the room for the speech's entirety.

First he discusses the same question that dogged Alfred Smith in his 1928 presidential campaign and John F. Kennedy in 1960: Does a Catholic have inappropriate loyalty to a foreign power — that is, the Pope? Here is where Bishop England is most emphatic.

" 'I would not allow,' he says, 'to the Pope or to any bishop of our Church, outside this Union, the smallest interference with the humblest vote at our most insignificant balloting box. He has no right to interference.' He then goes a step further by emphasizing that Congress and the U.S. government have

no right to meddle in the affairs of the Church. He told the gathering, 'You have no power to interfere with my religious rights, the tribunal of the Church has no power to interfere with my civil rights. It is a duty which every good man ought to discharge for his own, and for the public benefit, to resist any encroachment upon either.' Unfortunately, he notes, there are misinformed people who believe certain slanders against the Catholic Church. One is that the Church is despotic and antithetical to a republican form of government. He counters by citing Catholic individuals and nations who have been bulwarks against despotism, and argues that there is no evidence that Catholics are anything but true republican patriots.

"To the charge that the Church has encouraged persecution, he says that, sadly, every Church has practiced some degree of cruelty and bigotry. This was wrong, but there is nothing in Catholic teaching which encourages it. Even the Inquisition, he notes, was a civil, not a religious, movement."[48]

A cold January in Washington, D.C. Bishop John England became the first member of the Catholic clergy to address the United States Congress on January 8, 1826. Photo by author.

In the most humble, sincere, and succinct tones, the eloquent bish-op had diffused nearly every indictment against the coexistence of the Catholic Church and the rights of a democracy. He went on to clarify the role of Catholics in other governments relating the fear of over-throwing kings. Past European revolutions had been attributed to Papal interference.

> *"The final political point he addressed dealt with the Church's role in deposing unfriendly kings — clearly a practice that would raise concerns. The evidence, he argues, is absent; and legends to the contrary are the product of biased writ-ers. 'It is not,' he stresses, 'a tenet of the Church that popes interfere with legitimate governments, whether kingdoms or republics.'"[49]*

After his speech, there were many in Congress impressed enough that they had asked for a copy of his notes. The entire speech was later published and given to all in attendance. For Catholics, he had estab-lished the separation of allegiance for religious and secular matters. In a matter of weeks, England took oath to become an American citizen. His commitment to America was formalized.

> *"An American citizen by choice and from adoption, I feel it to be my duty to contribute my humble efforts to sustain the character of our country."[50]*

Bishop John England was unafraid of defending the Catholic Faith in America, as his depth of courage to do so had been well tested in his native Ireland. His profound convictions stood true.

In 1829 Bishop England instituted the Sisters of Charity of Our Lady of Mercy, whose good works included education, a school for girls, the establishment and administration of an orphanage and ancillary centers to assist the less fortunate. Their Motherhouse remains in Charleston nearly two centuries later. Bishop England also summoned another order, the Ursulines from Ireland, for additional teaching responsibilities. *The Philosophical and Classical Seminary of Charleston*, which England established in 1832 to build the religion upon a seminary. Bishop England also taught at the seminary.[51]

His care for the oppressed gave more insight to his purposeful leadership of the southern church. He was attentive to the plight of the blacks, not only in the city of Charleston, but also in the three state diocese.

He was sent by the Vatican to Haiti in 1834 to seek an accord between that country and the Papacy. That accord, a 'concordat,' was eventually signed by his successor Legate, Bishop Joseph Roseti of St. Louis.[52] In all, he made two very difficult trips to Haiti, the last trip testing his health to a point of near death. When travel was, by its nature, arduous and subject to peril, Bishop England persisted with purpose.

> *"In the interests of his impoverished diocese he visited the chief towns and cities of the Union, crossed the ocean four times, sought aid from the Holy Father, the Propaganda[53], the Leopoldine Society of Vienna, and made appeals in Ireland, England, France, Italy, wherever he could obtain money, vestments, or books. After Easter, in 1841, he visited Europe for the last time. On the long and boisterous return voyage there was much sickness, and he became seriously ill through his constant attendance on others. Though very weak, notwithstanding, on his arrival in Philadelphia, he preached seventeen nights consecutively, also four nights in Baltimore. With his health broken and his strength almost exhausted, he promptly resumed his duties on his return to Charleston, where he died, sincerely mourned by men of every creed and every party. His apostolic zeal, saintly life, exalted character, profound learning, and matchless eloquence made him a model for Catholics and an ornament of his order."[54]*

At 5:00 on the morning of April 11th, 1842, that Bishop John England died. Platitudes came in from every quarter, well outside of Charleston.

His life had made a difference and his death would surely create an unfillable void. Bishop Francis P. Kenrick of Philadelphia arrived to officiate the Funeral Mass before throngs that had gathered well outside of the doors of St. Finbar's.

The testimony of the writers and the words of the subsequent eulogy extolled the magnificence of the great and humble man. They expressed the wide reference of his impact to other areas of life beyond his primary spiritual quest.

> "But if we were filled with sorrow, if the unhidden tear flowed at the recollection of the name, the services and virtues of this prelate, let them honor that memory by adhering to the faith, by frequenting the sacraments, by cultivating that universal charity with persons of all climes, denominations and conditions, which it was the great object of his life to see consummated; that his name was dear to humanity; that it was cherished by the philanthropist; that philosophy honored him; that patriotism cherished him – he appealed to them to bear witness. But it was his more meek and fitting province to exhibit him as connected with religion."[55]

> "Most of his writings were given to the public through the columns of the United States Catholic Miscellany, in the publication of which he was aided by his sister, a woman of many-sided ability and talents. His successor, Bishop Ignatius Reynolds, collected his various writings, which were published in five volumes at Baltimore, in 1849."[56]

> Joanna England predeceased her brother, dying in 1827 during a cholera epidemic. She had served him as a secretary, administrator, and editor of The Catholic Miscellany. Much lamented by brother John, she was buried at St. Finbar's graveyard. Her brother was buried next to her in 1842. Upon the bishop's later exhumation, it was discovered that

Joanna's casket had melded to that of her holy brother. It is presumed that the Great Charleston Fire of 1861 that destroyed the newly built Cathedral (completed 1854) melded the two copper caskets together. For this reason, the basement mausoleum that holds the remains of Bishop John England also holds the remains of his sister, Joanna. Joanna England is believed to be among the first lay females, if not the first, whose remains are contained in a Cathedral in the United States.

Bishop England's death was a sad event in 1842 Charleston. He was accorded reverence across the community, notably from non-Catholic admirers.

*"When Bishop John England, the author of Provincial Councils and the light of the American Hierarchy, died in Charleston on April 11, 1842, all the city's church bells tolled and all flags were set at half-mast."*57

The significance of this event should be elevated by the fact that no Charleston area Catholic church had bells in 1842.

Bishop England's writing skills were a constant throughout his life. In recognition of his many journalistic efforts, the Catholic Press Association presents an annual publisher's award in his name.[58] His oratory skills were heard well beyond the Holy City, as well.

England inspired others. He changed Charleston. He strengthened a three-state diocese in the South, where Catholicism was a missionary undertaking. He also laid foundations of insight and communication concerning Catholicism that permanently altered the Church's standing in America to one of great respect.

CHAPTER SIX

O'BRIEN'S ENGLAND:

The Apostle to Democracy

The refreshing and substantive account rendered by Monsignor Joseph Laurence O'Brien in his extensive 1934 publication titled *John England, Bishop of Charleston: Apostle to Democracy* studies the major aspects of England's 21-year episcopate.

The work of Father O'Brien went well beyond the research and publication of this work. Indeed, it may be surmised that there was not a latter day biographer outside of Catholic University's Dr. Peter Guilday who studied more about the famous first Charleston Bishop. Father O'Brien's contributions to the Diocese of Charleston are quite considerable and will be explored in the subsequent chapters of this work. For now, we will focus on his insightful historic assessment of the brilliance of Bishop John England through the late Monsignor Joseph Laurence O'Brien, another priest of high eloquence.

Portrait of Monsignor Joseph Laurence O'Brien
Phot courtesy Diocese of Charleston.

O'Brien deftly cites the early Bishop's strengths and successes. He uses much of what was available to him in his research, including a personal diary Bishop England began in 1821, the week after his Charleston arrival. Topics included England's patriotic exuberance for his adopted America, his journalistic endeavors to include *The United States Catholic Miscellany*, his personal letters, his determined defense of the Catholic Faith, and his role as a teacher. He further explores the role Bishop England played in following the tenets of democracy in the institution of the Catholic Church in America.

> *"It is clear that for responsible dissent, for a Catholic Constitution, for democratic Catholic Conventions, for National Councils of the Catholic Church – in short, for the employment of participatory decision-making, of democracy as it flows from the American civil experience in the life of*

> *the Catholic Church – Bishop John England of Charleston,*
> *South Carolina, provides a premier precedent."*[59]

O'Brien also cites England's resolve in the defense of the Catholic faith as a major credit to his timely leadership. He took it upon himself to graciously answer every challenger.

One long-running letter campaign was a display of John England's intellect. The repartee was reprinted in an 1849 edited collection of letters by Bishop Ignatius Reynolds of Charleston. The point-counter-point exchange began in July of 1839 when a former Episcopal Priest turned Baptist Minister, Richard Fuller, defended the planned placement of anti-Catholic script on a proposed monument.

Fuller was a gifted orator and had been championed as one of the fine debators of his day. First in his class at Harvard, Fuller became a Beaufort lawyer before devoting his life to religion. His staunch support of slavery by debate and letters was instrumental in the divide of the American Baptist Church into Southern and Northern Baptist Conventions.[60] His argument against Catholics stirred the public sentiment, inciting response – which Bishop John England so adequately fulfilled.

England was deeply devoted to defending the Catholic faith as he felt there were many misgivings and erroneous arguments assaulting it for too long. The exchanges between the two scholars were diatribes researched and positioned as nearly endless rebuttals. These assertions and responses were each reprinted in *The Charleston Courier* as the public became enamored with the excellent high-level debate.

Nearly as remarkable as the zeal in their discourse is the genuine esteem these two religious men had cited for each other in the exchange. The polite dialogue initiated each letter, the salutation being equally complimentary. In the end, the Reverend Fuller and Bishop England became friends – mostly built upon mutual respect.

The defense of the separation of church and state, which England had supported in his speech before the U.S. House of Representatives in January of 1826, did much to elevate England as the most respected episcopate of his time.

Monsignor O'Brien's careful treatment and preservation of the Bishop John England legacy, written twenty years after O'Brien's arrival in Charleston, had other impact than to render a biographical work. O'Brien's publication was distributed as a fine biography and a meticulously researched source material. The key argument for the separation of church and state had been made by England. It would be used one hundred years later to develop political careers for two boys who attended parochial schools in Charleston.

Indeed, a student of St. Patrick School, James Francis 'Jimmy' Byrnes, would become Governor of South Carolina, Secretary of State, and Secretary of War (during World War II). Another St. Patrick School student, John P. Grace, would become the first Catholic mayor of Charleston. Monsignor O'Brien, a friend and mentor to the mayor, performed the mayor's eulogy at the Cathedral of St. John the Baptist in June of 1940.

O'Brien explores Bishop England's foray into higher education. Having studied law at Carlow, followed by theology, England was a well-educated prelate. He was most willing to share his knowledge with Catholics and non-Catholics alike. O'Brien takes the reader through England's educational background to introduce his intention of building the faith through proper education. He did this through the founding of several educational institutions to include the School for Free Blacks, the Philosophical Society, and the Seminary. He taught at every opportunity at places well outside of the Cathedral pulpit.

O'Brien also researched the private letters and daily journal of the bishop. Bishop England often wrote to his family in Ireland. He wrote to Rome and to Washington. He continually promoted his idea for a bishop's conference through the Archdiocese of Baltimore. He wrote personal appeals for funding and requested support clergy. He asked sisters to assist in schools, hospitals, and orphanages – founding an order, The Sisters of Charity of Our Lady of Mercy in 1829.

The founding of *The United States Catholic Miscellany* gave America the first such periodical and established an informative messenger of the Catholic Faith that reached well beyond homiletic expression. With the help of England's sister, Joanna, this newspaper helped define the early years of Catholicity in the United States.

In the choosing of Bishop England as the high school name, Monsignor O'Brien provided a reminder of one of America's most important early Catholic personalities. He presented a genuine and heroic patron of the Catholic Church who had dedicated his life to the advancement of Christian values, secular freedoms, and public discourse.

Beyond O'Brien's volume, several other biographical depictions of Bishop John England were published, including the edited collection of letters of Bishop England by his successor, Bishop Ignatius Russell (1849), *The Works of the Right Reverend John England, First Bishop of Charleston*. Other works by Sebastian G. Messmer, Archbishop of Milwaukee, were published in seven volumes (1908). *The Life and Times of John England 1786-1842*, by Dr. Peter Guilday, is in two volumes and serves as a testament of Bishop John England's two-continent endeavors, before and after his arrival in America. It was published in 1927. The fascination with the subject of Bishop John England remains.

CHAPTER SEVEN

POINT COUNTER POINT

The extraordinary width of John England's life has to be considered within his times, though his intellect and conviction transcended his era. England made four Atlantic crossings when navigation was upon the heavens and the wind and currents, though somewhat predictable, were yet inexact. The large masted ships were not as comfortable ocean liners are today. Sleeping quarters were cramped and foods were not available as fresh or well preserved.

England traveled inland, mostly by horse-drawn carriage, on roads that were dirt corridors subject to the vagaries of weather. He stayed with families, mostly, as there were not hotels in many of the small communities.

Given these conditions, it becomes more astonishing to subtract the travel time away from his life's accomplishment. He would not have been able to write letters during land transit, nor deliver letters during ocean transit. Yet he was a man of voluminous correspondence, diary entries, and regularly published material. He wrote, delivered, and preserved his speeches. Until the age of electricity many decades after his time, it was very difficult to produce such works in the evening hours. Yet, it could be concluded that John England was a man of letters.

What has written about Bishop John England over nearly two centuries edifies the fascination of this holy man who worked tirelessly within his convictions. England wrote and spoke consistently upon these convictions. Yet, he is measured beyond his time by a few biographers to some detriment because of this consistency. For instance, England believed that the democracy in America was a shining example to the world and some of its tenets would best be applied the to process that the Papacy utilized in the appointment of new bishops.

> *"The Sees of Boston and New York are now vacant, or if Prelates have been appointed for them, I am not aware of who they are. They will both be filled before I shall probably address you upon the necessity of having some permanent and known mode of having our Sees filled, not by faction, intrigue or accident - but in a manner more likely to be useful and satisfactory than that which is now in operation."*[61]

Obviously, this did not endear England to the hierarchy of the Roman Catholic Church, but it did reinforce his organizational mindset of what he considered a much better and more appropriate process.

His call for a council of bishops in the United States to meet regularly was not endorsed by the French-born Archbishop Ambrose Marèchal, but was indeed an organizational nuance that advanced the church in America. It was not until Archbishop Marèchal's death in 1828 that England was able to convince his successor, Archbishop James Whitfield, of the need for these councils. The conjectural resilience and perhaps jealousy of other bishops followed, as in his times of arduous travel, a council of this magnitude may have been quite unpopular. After several iterations, the idea and form followed and the first Provincial Council of Bishops met in Baltimore in 1829.[62] England's enthusiasm for these meetings served other purposes, as well.

England also advocated conventions for the clergy and laity as part of his constitution for the Diocese of Charleston. He believed that the Catholic Church was primarily 'catholic,' far-reaching and for all to benefit. Other bishops did not follow, and some in fact, wrote to Rome to warn of the practice of diocesan constitutions. Nonetheless, the benefits proved to be consistent with the purpose of building a lasting foundation for the Catholic Church in the American South. The diocesan conventions also served another historical function.

> *"Consequently his 26 Convention Addresses give a history of the Catholic Church in America for those years. Most importantly, it was through the Convention that the scattered Catholic churches began to grow together with a sense of unity and belonging to a larger church, a "catholic" Church, which was their Church where they had both rights and responsibilities."*[63]

In the inspection of England's perceived need for a constitution, it appears that his attained enthusiasm for the United States Constitution and the Bill of Rights was applied to the concern over vestries. The lay vestries had been a catalyst for his ordination and assignment to Charleston. In England's opinion, what was written as law in America followed as the form of governance. Thus, he wrote and published a constitution for the three-state diocese and submitted it to Rome.

The new campus of Bishop England High School advances the precepts of Monsignor J.L. O'Brien's vision of spirituality, academia, and physical fitness. Photo by Author.

*"But the people desire to have the Constitution printed, so
that they may have a standard by which they may be guided.
I have learned by experience that the genius of this nation is
to have written laws at hand, and to direct all their affairs
according to them. If this be done, they are easily governed.
If this be refused, a long and irremediable contention will
ensue."*[64]

Though respectful of all others, Bishop England had gained a wide
reputation for his intellectual oration and outspoken stance on myriad
issues. American slavery was taken to task, though he resided in the port
that imported more slaves than any other in the United States. Pundits
point that England did not change slavery or become a martyr for the
cause of abolition. Yet, the evidence of his strong remarks against the
prevailing tide in the American South, in a city that became the kindling of the bonfire that was the American Civil War, leave no doubt
to his conviction. In fact, he took noteworthy action. On the issue, it
should be considered that he was sent to Charleston with the primary
goal of establishing the Catholic Church in the American South. He
did that. Along the way, the most volatile issue he encountered was the
abolition of slavery. He had arrived from a country that advocated one
culture, the British, controlling another, the Irish. He lived the injustice
in his native Cork. England never shied from the discussion and his
position that slavery would eventually become abolished, as it did not
reconcile within the democratic principles of America's founding. He
was ultimately correct, but historically in the wrong place and era.

Though the good bishop was widely admired inside his faith and
upon nearly every periphery, he was not averse to controversy. His consistency was based in the democratic principles he admired. His life's
work can best be assessed by the impact of his organizational institutions
well beyond his fifty-six years.

Chapter Eight

THEY CALLED
HIM "DOC"

I t is rare that a person arrives in a community and becomes an immediate agent of progress – a guide for a new age. When the tall and slender Joseph Laurence O'Brien arrived in Charleston at the age of 28, he made an abrupt impact upon the life of numerous Charlestonians – well beyond the sphere of Catholicity. The youthful and athletic Catholic Priest was well equipped to the tasks he had anticipated.

Like Bishop John England, Father O'Brien inventoried the resources and considered what was absent as much as what was available. There were definitive educational needs evident in Charleston – resources he knew well in the burgeoning Catholic population of Scranton, Pennsylvania – the area that propelled his spiritual upbringing. Scranton and the area nearby had the Catholic formula for growth – parochial schools, convents, hospitals, and two seminaries (St. Charles Borromeo and St. Vincent). The Irish and German immigration to the area supported an eleven-county Diocese of Scranton, established in 1868.[65]

Father O'Brien's pre-Charleston existence was immersed in the Americana and Catholic life he enjoyed in the small town of Avoca, less than ten miles from Scranton.

"Msgr. Joseph L. 'Doc' O'Brien was born 30 April 1884 in Avoca, Pa., to Thomas F. O'Brien and Sarah A. Morahan.

His mother was born in England. O'Brien had three brothers and two sisters. He attended Mount St. Mary's Seminary in Emmitsburg, Md., and the Albertinum seminary in Fribourg, Switzerland. Advanced degrees include M.A., S.T.D., and L.L.D."[66]

Father O'Brien became a Monsignor in 1934.[67] His nickname 'Doc' may have had Avoca roots, though later students suggested that it came from his first honorary doctorate degree. Nonetheless, he was comfortable with the name in deference to the formality of "Monsignor."

O'Brien was a seminarian for the Diocese of Scranton (Pa.). Bishop Henry Northrop adopted O'Brien for the Diocese of Charleston in 1910. He was ordained in Fribourg (Switzerland) on the 15th of December 1912.[68] The selection of Charleston suited young Father O'Brien, who had long admired and studied the first bishop of Charleston, John England. In many ways, Bishop England was a guide to the young priest's pastoral aspirations.

O'Brien served at Cathedral of St. John the Baptist (Charleston, S.C.) from 1914-1929. He was co-founder (with Father James J. May) of Bishop England High School and served as its rector from its beginning in 1915 until 1947. O'Brien became Pastor to St. Patrick Parish (Charleston, S.C.) in 1929.[69]

The young priest was a busy man. He traveled to Avoca nearly every summer to visit his family, but made the experience productive by teaching literature courses at Marywood College Summer School. He also taught religion and literature courses at the convent of the Sisters of Saints Cyril and Methodius in Danville, Pennsylvania.[70]

His eloquent delivery from the pulpit attracted non-parishioners and friends from across the Charleston community. He was a much-admired banquet speaker as well as a weekly media personality on WCSC radio, a venue for his resonant voice.

His talent for organization and operational strategies became most apparent in his challenging mission of beginning a new high school. But the high school was but one of his brick and mortar projects. He was also responsible for the construction of a brick parochial school building on St. Philip Street for St. Patrick's Parish, and, later, the renovation of St. Patrick's church and rectory. The original red brick church had been built in 1879.[71] The formation of the high school in 1915 was the first step in a process. The permanent high school was built on Calhoun Street in 1921, completed in time for enrollment in the fall of 1922. The replacement high school at Daniel Island was completed seventy-six years later.

Bishop England High School campus 1917-1998. Photo courtesy Bishop England High School.

It should be noted that Father O'Brien's construction projects took place at times considered inopportune – during World War I and into the years of the Great Depression. Though Father O'Brien arrived in Charleston nearly a century after Bishop John England, he performed these tasks as if he were extending Bishop England's vision for Charleston. The newly arrived priest had become a major catalyst for advancing Catholic education to the high school level, as he had known its impact upon Scranton.

O'Brien's emulation of the famous first Bishop, John England, became evident in literature. He wrote a biography of the man he felt changed

America as the most important episcopate of his time *–John England, Bishop of Charleston, The Apostle to Democracy.* It was published in 1934.

The first bishop and the inventive priest had much in common. Like Bishop England, O'Brien was a fearless innovator. A tall man of formidable presence, he brought a sense of apostolic community from his parochial experiences in Pennsylvania. In Charleston, the primary schools existed – ostensibly by the work of the Sisters of Charity of Our Lady of Mercy whom Bishop John England introduced to the Diocese. Just as England introduced four sisters in support of primary schools and an orphanage, Father O'Brien recommended additional outside support of religious orders. The high school would need several priests and sisters to teach. By moving Catholic learning to the next level, he also encroached upon the nuance of a co-educational environment. This concept at the high school level was previously a non-starter, even in public schools, in post-Reconstruction Charleston. The societal precepts of the Victorian Age (1837-1901) had cast its shadow upon this innovation.

The lower schools existed in 1914 at Cathedral, St. Patrick's and St. Joseph parishes, and the latter two maintained coeducational status. The Academy of Our Lady of Mercy provided elementary and secondary education for girls only.[72] The Academy was administered in the building still in use as the Neighborhood House on North Hampstead Square in Charleston. It was the design of Architect Albert Wheeler Todd.[73]

There was little doubt that the high school should be named to honor his personal religious model, Bishop John England. The permanent naming of the high school occurred in the second academic year, 1916-1917.

The first location of the new high school was simply attached to the See of the Diocese, the Cathedral of St. John the Baptist. The new high school was designated as 'Cathedral High School.' It convened in the auxiliary Cathedral school building, once used as the church while funds were being raised to rebuild the previous edifice. That first year effort placed 67 students in four grades – the 7th, 9th, 10th and 11th.[74] The absence of 8th grade students is not explained, though an eighth grade appeared the following year. It was not until 1948 that the high school added the twelfth grade. Owing to this nuance, there was no graduating class in 1947.

The Diocese did not have to contemplate long for an appropriate naming of the new Catholic High School. The introduction of Father O'Brien's highest recommendation: 'Bishop John England Memorial High School,' was forwarded to Bishop Russell in 1916. Time and convenience unofficially redacted the naming elements of 'John' and 'Memorial' to simply Bishop England High School.[75]

In Monsignor O'Brien's own words from his work entitled "John England, A Man of God, he narrates the reason for the naming of the high school after the first bishop.

> *"…when the Bishop England High School was in the dangerous days of its infancy, the writer (Monsignor O'Brien) was walking on the Battery with one deeply concerned with the affairs for the Church in South Carolina. Quite unexpectedly, he said to me: 'Father, tell me something if you don't mind. Why did you name the high school the Bishop England High School?' I'll summarize my answer.*

> *"John England was the first writer or speaker to make the Catholic religion respectable in the estimation of the American public. He restored classical learning in South Carolina. He established the first Catholic weekly journal in the United States. He edited an edition of the Missal for use among his people and revised the catechism in a manner suitable to their needs. He founded the Sisters of Our Lady of Mercy. He was, in his lifetime, the greatest apologist and is yet the greatest apologist the United States has known. He was a preacher of such magnetism that Protestant churches vied with one another to grant him the use of their pulpits.*

"He taught us how to appreciate the Protestant position and charted for us the workings of the anti-Catholic mind. He taught us how to organize Catholic Action.

"When he was chosen bishop, he was considered by the Congregation of the Propagation of the Faith the most courageous, the most zealous, the most eloquent of his contemporaries. As a bishop, up to the hour of his death, he was the most courageous, the most zealous, the most eloquent member of the American Hierarchy. And to this day, I am convinced that he still remains the most courageous, the most zealous, the most eloquent bishop the United States has known. I hope the school will become the monument worthy of his genius."[76]

The quest to advance Catholic education and to supply the region with well-trained students within the discipline of the Catholic Faith became the focus of Father O'Brien. He was determined to recruit assistance from others for the benefit of all.

In a request to Mrs. Ida Ryan in New York, Father O'Brien mentioned the second-year enrollment of 82 "with room to grow to 150 students." Father O'Brien asked for other support to grow the school, settling on a need of $2000. Mrs. Ryan had previously donated the former home for the Cenacle Sisters near Calhoun and Pitt Streets for the interim use of the high school.

Unfortunately, Mrs. Ryan declined in a terse response letter dated April 19, 1917.

"Rev. dear Fr. O'Brien,
Am sorry but have on hand all I can undertake.
Yours sincerely,
Ida M. Ryan,
Suffern, NY."

The letter to Mrs. Ryan mentioned the faculty – five sisters at $20 per month each, and three teaching priests who were unpaid. Importantly, he noted his dream for the school – that it become an endowed institution.

On March 17th of 1916, Father O'Brien presented one of the great American orators of his day, Bourke Cochran, to address the Catholics of Charleston about the importance of a Catholic education. Cochran, after some juxtaposing of schedule, became the Hibernian Society banquet speaker for the evening, with festivities of St. Patrick's Day surrounding the event. Tickets were sold for fifty cents, reserved seats for 75 cents. The Hibernian Society postponed its annual banquet dinner until 9:30 that evening to give its membership the opportunity to hear Bourke Cochran.[77]

US Congressman W. Bourke Cochran
Photo Courtesy Library of Congress

Retired Confederate Colonel James Armstrong, who was himself described by Confederate General Robert E. Lee as 'the bravest man he ever knew,' introduced Congressman Cochran. Armstrong was serving as the President of the Hibernian Society. Cochran's lecture title, listed in the O'Brien family archival documents was, "St. Patrick, the Effect of his Mission on the Revival of Letters."[78]

Cochran, born in Ireland's County Sligo, had become an American citizen and was elected to five non-consecutive terms in the U.S. Congress. He was said to have once dated Winston Churchill's mother and, later, mentored young Winston on the art of public speaking. Cochran was also considered largely responsible for the close election of President William McKinley as United States President in 1896.[79] As one considered among the finest orators of his day, he gave Father O'Brien and the Diocese of Charleston much needed momentum in their quest to build a new high school.

In other notes, Father O'Brien gives much credit to the Cochran speech of 1916 as the major persuasion to the Catholics of Charleston for the importance of a Catholic high school. But the collection plate had to be passed outside of the church aisles.

Indeed, money had to be raised, a curriculum chosen, discipline established, and a faculty assembled. The second year of the high school brought upon new challenges.

In a letter circulated in 1916 to the parents of the students, he wrote

> *"For the first time in the history of Charleston, an open air Mass will be celebrated."*

Bishop William T. Russell (1917-1929
Photo Courtesy Diocese of Charleston

Bishop William T. Russell presided at the closing ceremonies on the school grounds for the first year at Calhoun Street, on June 17th, 1917, at 5:30 p.m. Bishop Russell was most supportive of the new high school.

The correspondence of Monsignor O'Brien gives compelling testimony to his educational and vocational insights. Twenty-two Catholic men signed a pledge to raise funds as necessary for the support of the first year on Calhoun Street (the second year of the high school). They sought two hundred subscribers at $10 each to defray the expected annual cost of operating the school – only $2000. The initial group of students included fifty-four boys and thirteen girls in the first year. There were eighty-one enrolled in the second year.

It is noteworthy that in the face of his proposition that the high school be co-educational, Father O'Brien took another great risk. Catholics, and others, were loath to have their daughters attend the same school as boys, with profound concern for proper oversight. Father O'Brien assured parents that he would assume the direct responsibility. There were no contemporary co-educational high schools in Charleston. However, Catholic boys and girls attended co-educational parish elementary schools since 1906.

Father O'Brien thought it important to impose the guidelines of restraint, as he felt necessary. On January 10th, 1917, he issued a circular to the parents of the co-educational high school students. The circular was also published in the *Charleston News and Courier*.

It advised parents against the two social concerns of the day – movies and dancing. Movies were in their infancy as black and white action film without voices, interrupted by the post of a placard reciting what was to be said or thought. "Talkies" were not in theaters until a full decade later![80]

In dancing, the Tango had already arrived, but the new craze was dancing to Jazz.[81] Father O'Brien warned the parents.

> *"The age is amusement mad, and not mad on healthy amusement; and a boy or a girl who is going to resist this spirit must have an excellently formed character… To come to the point,*

*there are two great dangers which confront your sons and
your daughters – two great dangers which have already un-
dermined the moral nature of many boys and girls, and your
boy and your girl may be the next. And both you and I will
fail in our duty unless we shield them by word and example.
What are these dangers? <u>DANCING</u> for boys and girls who
are at the formative ages, and <u>MOVING</u> <u>PICTURES,</u> which
are poisoning their imagination and visualizing refined sin
before their eyes. Already I hear objections…but if you and
I hope to win out we must smash down these objections."*[82]

He was way ahead of his time in his daily observations. The century
beyond plunged impressionable children into many more 'mad amuse-
ments.' Surely he would have written about edgy satirical cartoons, vio-
lent action movies, and the preponderance of social media, among other
cultural 'advances'!

The entire faculty was comprised of Monsignor O'Brien, his assis-
tant, Father James J. May (for whom the present-day May Forest Convent
Home on James Island is named), and four sisters of The Sisters of Charity
of Our Lady of Mercy, founded by Bishop John England."[83]

In 1921, while the original building on Calhoun Street was being
razed, BEHS rented space at Gregorian Hall on George Street.

The cornerstone of the new main building in 1921, noted the hierar-
chal authorities listed in the O'Brien notes: "Pope Benedict XV, President
Warren G. Harding, Governor R.A. Cooper, Mayor John P. Grace" and
the then-Bishop of Charleston, William T. Russell.[84] The new high
school was dedicated to "Saint Paul, the Apostle of the Gentiles."[85]

Father O'Brien embarked upon a major fundraising campaign.
For this, he needed wide diocesan support and an expert fundraising
accomplice.

The Catholic population in Charleston remained small. Yet, it was
imperative that substantial funds were raised among this community for
the establishment of the new high school in its permanent site of 1922.
For that task, Father O'Brien recruited the very capable Father James

J. May. Father May was another outstanding communicator, but more importantly, he was a taskmaster. Together, Fathers O'Brien and May began a plan that would become a modern high school that would reach into Charleston's future.

While Father O'Brien carefully detailed his timing and strategy in raising $50,000 needed to build the new high school and to also furnish the rooms with desks, chairs and teaching aids within the grand total, he needed key assistance.

Father James May
Photo Courtesy Diocese of Charleston.

Father James J. May (1887-1958)[86] was charged with the responsibility of organizing the fundraising for the new high school. May, who had been ordained in 1913, later served St. Francis Xavier Infirmary as the lead fundraiser for its addition in 1926. He became the Director of Catholic Charities for the Diocese and the Director of Catholic Cemeteries. He served as Rector of the Cathedral Parish from 1928 to 1950. Much beloved, he made many selfless contributions to the Charleston community and beyond. May assisted Monsignor O'Brien with renovations to St. Patrick's Church and helped raise funds for the Wood Memorial School. May also performed admirably in support of American troops during both World War I and World War II. Notably, he led the fundraising effort for the new convent for the Sisters of Charity of Our Lady of Mercy, a beautiful site that bares his name, May Forest on James Island. Elevated to Monsignor in 1934, May was selected as Vicar General of the Diocese of Charleston.[87]

Father May showed a skillful exuberance for the task of encouraging the funding for the new high school. He devised a plan to inspire teams of Catholics from across the city. He incorporated two competing teams – thirteen teams of ladies and ten teams of men. Typically, each team had seven members. The early twentieth century Charleston names emerged from these lists – Molony, Croghan, Schachte, McCarthy, Hartnett, O'Neill, Budds, LeTellier, Trouche, Devereux, Lighthart, Duffy, Grace, Erickson, Matson, Furlong, McAlister, Moran, Comar, Rooney, Dengate, Storen, Igoe, Beshere, Albenesius, Maguire, Hollings, Jarvis, Murphy, Gibson and Lowry. One could recognize these early names evolving as yet more street names, buildings, and prominent businesses a century later. Mrs. J.J. Furlong chaired the women's effort. Mr. M.A. Condon chaired the men's division. Mr. A.W. Litschgi was named as the general chairman for the entire project by Father O'Brien.[88]

Of those early contributors listed, so many became highly recognized Charleston families many decades later – Riley, Condon, Magrath, Oliver, Burmester, Leonard, Brandt, Cosgrove, Brennan, Sottile, Cantwell, Souberoux, Michel, Aimar, Bouvette, Hanley, Bicaise, Barbot, and Livingston. These Charleston names endured. Some are associated with place names that have emerged from them or their progeny – Cosgrove Avenue, Riley Park, Sottile Theater, etc.

Knights of Columbus Council 704
Photo by Author.

The fundraising teams met monthly at the new Knights of Columbus Hall on Calhoun Street, whose listed building committee from 1908 reveals many of the same names. Meetings would include remarks from speakers that reminded the fundraisers of why they were building a high school that taught religion. One speech by a businessman spoke to the need of properly trained women to type and take shorthand notes, pointing out that the Charleston businesses would hire them upon the completion of their coursework.

The Rev. P.N. Lynch Council 704 hosted these monthly fundraising meetings, usually with a meal and a speaker at the expansive Knights of Columbus Hall. One monthly speaker, Rev. Father Hyland, reminded the assemblage in June of 1919, "You are preparing the greatest defense of our nation."[89] He warned with a tale about a country without higher education that would fall prey to those educated. His speech was a post World War I message that warned of future wars.

The fundraising reports summed $84,118. It was well more than the $50,000 goal that had been since adjusted up to $75,000. The reports showed that the ladies obtained more donors and the men more funds. There were significant funds raised amongst non-Catholics – again by some foundation names of the community – Pringle, Marjenhoff, Solomon, McDowell, Patrick, Faber, Cotton, Young, Blalock and Van Smith.[90]

Upon completion of construction for the new school, Bishop Russell officiated at the ceremony that opened the school. Bishop Russell's comments that day extolled the work of Father O'Brien and the Catholics of Charleston.

> *"Our High School is completed. It was built by the hardearned money of the Catholics of this Diocese. It is out of debt," Bishop Russell began.*

> *"When the passerby asks what building this is in the heart of Charleston, surrounded by its spacious grounds, and is told that it is a Catholic high school, he will conclude that the Catholics of Charleston appreciate higher education. It will be evident that those who planned, worked for, and completed this undertaking are determined that their children shall have an opportunity to make themselves something more than hewers of wood and drawers of water.*

> *"Facts are stubborn things. This institution is a fact. We have dreamed of it, and sometimes in the past, a high school was in the planning. Today it is a fact. When I first proposed to build a high school for $36,000, I was told it is impossible. With willing hands and loving hearts nothing is impossible. You have placed in my hands not merely the money I asked, but you have completed a high school of sixteen rooms, including an assembly hall capable of accommodating three hundred, at a cost of more than $56,000; and, besides, you*

have borne the expense of running the old high school for two years. Altogether, since you have put your shoulders to the wheel, you have, besides supporting your three parochial schools and the convent, contributed to education through this high school about $65,000.

"The credit for beginning this high school in Charleston belongs to Father O'Brien. He planned it, he worked for it, he made it such a success that you bravely tore down the old building on this site and determined to erect a new high school that would be worthy of its director, the Sisters, the children, and the education that was given in this institution.

"The Catholics of Charleston can never be too grateful to Fr. O'Brien for what he has done for their children."[91]

Father O'Brien set the curriculum. Every student studied Latin. Each student had five classes per week in Religion, specifically studying the New Testament. The 'commercial' courses were typing, stenography, and penmanship. Five classes per week were given in Math and English, and another five split with American History and Geography. No class had more than 12 students. By the year's end, eleven students had left, reasons not given.[92]

An interesting note found in the O'Brien family papers from July 5th of 1916 gives insight to Father O'Brien's demanding curriculum and those that would and would not meet the requirements.

"If an honor roll were published it would contain most of the names of those enrolled. We refrain from publishing the names of those who failed in class work or in conduct, in as much as such publication would serve no good purpose."[93]

Father O'Brien preferred the optimism of a positive result.

Founding the high school furthered the education of young people into two distinct course areas – the commercial business field and the classical learning field. As O'Brien progressed within the new assignment, he also participated in assisting others in other communities.

Between 1943 and 1945, Monsignor O'Brien served the state and the country at the National Conference of Christians and Jews.[94] These conferences were performed at U.S. military camps and Army Air bases with the charge to forge better understandings among those fighting for freedoms and the American way of life.

As radio became a popular mode of communication, Monsignor O'Brien worked with a local station, WCSC to host a Sunday program. By testimony from his contemporaries, it was a show not to be missed. His resonant voice, according to one former student and program listener, Walter Duane, was both forceful and full of encouragement.

Father O'Brien also served the Diocese of Charleston as the Superintendent of Catholic Schools. This effort produced measurable growth in parochial school building throughout the state, bringing the benefit of parochial education to the growing cities of Columbia and Greenville.

His later years were spent at the rectory of St. Patrick's Church, where he had resided since 1929. There, he was able to write daily letters to former students, friends, and family. He died there on the morning of March 2nd, 1952, at the age of 67. The Mass of Christian Burial and subsequent interment was well attended. The size of the crowd forced authorities to close St. Phillips Street for the duration of the service. A much-loved holy man had passed from the earth.

Chapter Nine

TWO PRIESTS OF CHARLESTON

Through the study of Bishop John England, and with the help of Dr. Peter Guilday's works, and that of Monsignor O'Brien in his family papers, some comparisons are imminent.

Both Bishop England and Monsignor O'Brien had a sister that became a nun and a brother who became a priest. Bishop England's sister remained in Ireland. Though the Bishop had an additional sister, Joanna, who dedicated much of her life to the Bishop's assistance. His brother, Thomas R. England, served a parish at Passage West (Cork) until he died from the Irish Famine in 1847. He was cherished for his caring of the prisoners of Spike Island (a jail much like San Francisco's Alcatraz) in Cork harbor.

Bishop England's sister, Mary England, was a brilliant student and teacher. She entered the North Presentation Convent in 1811 – the very same convent where her brother John served nearly ten years as chaplain. She took the name Sister Catherine from 'St. Catherine of Siena.' The North Presentation Convent in Cork remained her home until her death in 1872, thirty years after her brother's death in Charleston. Bishop England returned to Ireland three times (1832, 1834 and 1841). It was an express command of Cork's Bishop Murphy that disallowed Sister Catherine England from joining her brother in Charleston in the year

1834. Sister Catherine led a dedicated life of teaching and tending to the sick. She was versed in Latin, French, Spanish, German, and Greek.[95]

Father O'Brien's brother, William, became a priest and served a parish in Brooklyn, NY. Sister Mary Gerald O'Brien entered the OLM Community in 1916 and served the diocese until her death in 1984.[96] Father O'Brien's only other brother, Tommy, followed Father O'Brien to Charleston and assisted him. He eventually married and moved to Columbia, SC. It is from the descendants of the Columbia family of brother Thomas O'Brien that many of the 2014 private family documents and letters have been preserved.

These non-contemporaneous church leaders, England and O'Brien, left significant impressions upon their admiring contemporaries and a lasting heritage to their diocese. There were other obvious similarities.

Both Bishop England and Father O'Brien were ordained abroad, England taking Holy Orders in Cork, Ireland; O'Brien receiving his Holy Orders in Fribourg, Switzerland. Both came to Charleston as part of a 'missionary' status, since Catholicism was only about 1% of the diocesan population of their era. Both were responsible for recruiting holy women. Bishop England founded the Sisters of Charity of Our Lady of Mercy (1829) and further recruited the Ursuline Order. Monsignor O'Brien needed teaching assistance from outside of the Diocese of Charleston. Bishop Russell agreed and the Sisters of Saints Cyril and Methodius responded, and later the Oblate Sisters of Providence. Both England and O'Brien served as teachers and professors, each at the college level. Both were authors, the Bishop as a constant contributor to periodicals in his native Ireland and, later, as founder of *The United States Catholic Miscellany*. Monsignor O'Brien penned many contributions to journals and wrote his life's work in 1934, *John England, Bishop of Charleston, Apostle to Democracy*. Their homilies and public addresses are much preserved for other ages. Both were non-adversarial personalities, extending sincere courtesies to others outside of the Catholic faith. Both exhibited brave leadership within firm principles by their profound convictions. They were both considered academics with a propensity for research and enlightenment. Both were masters of organizational procedures (preferring to recruit people towards a common strategy).

The legacy that was Father O'Brien has breached a century through the trifold mission of spirituality, academic prowess, and physical growth for the high school he named. The forging of the brand Catholic in the Diocese of Charleston was a die cast by the Corkman, Bishop John England. Through the efforts of Father O'Brien and Father James J. May, the strength of that educational component metal has held true.

Bishop England High School became one of the elite athletic
high schools in America.
Photo Courtesy Bishop England School Library.

In its natural progression, it should be noted that other selfless priests have also made monumental contributions, each in their own style to the tremendous benefit of the high school. These include a most devout Reverend John L. Manning (as Rector, 1947 to 1959), the tall and resonant orator, Reverend William J. Croghan (1959 to 1964), the personable Monsignor Robert J. Kelly (as Rector, 1964 – 1990) and the incomparable wit and insight exhibited by Monsignor Laurence B. McInerny throughout his stint as Rector, which began in 1990.

Proudly, Bishop England High School was the first integrated high school in the State of South Carolina and featured the first South Carolina High School League minority athlete in the person of Arthur McFarland, who graduated with honors and furthered his education at the University of Notre Dame and the Law School at the University of Virginia, returning to Charleston to eventually become a municipal judge, among other accomplishment. Other quite notable graduates include the ten-term Mayor of Charleston, Joseph P. Riley, Jr., former United States Congressman Thomas F. Hartnett, along with the entrepreneurial mayor of the burgeoning Town of Mt. Pleasant, John J. Dodds, Jr. There are compelling numbers of more-than-notable graduates from varied fields and professions who have benefitted from the broad and enlightened Catholic education afforded at BEHS.

Bishop England High School has earned a wide spiritual, educational, and athletic reputation un-matched in South Carolina. The 100-Year result is to be both celebrated and appreciated. The alumni, students, parents, and faculty should be ever mindful of the sacrifices of its founders, the now eponymous names of John England and Joseph Laurence 'Doc' O'Brien, two priests who have built a lasting value enjoyed by many generations.

There are immutable laws of earth that cannot be violated. There is the law of gravity. There is life as well as death. There is time and mass, finite math – and irrefutable science. And there are secular laws that are supported by laws that God put forth. The Apostle Matthew writes of Christ's law. In Chapter 22, verses 37-40, He reveals:

> *"You shall love the Lord, your God, with all your heart, with all your soul, and with all your mind. This is the greatest and the first commandment. The second is like it: You shall love your neighbor as yourself. The whole law and the prophets depend on these two commandments."*

It is the love of Christ and love of their fellow man that is seen as thematic in the lives of both priests. Yet there were struggles. To make a mark of success, one must often overcome obstacles of the journey that may seem impassable.

For Bishop John England, adversity was his birthright. It commanded his early environment, wrought with the restrictions of a ruling class. He was further challenged with a large missionary state, more than five times the size of his home country. This vast territory became his diocese – in what was mostly a wilderness. He faced the bigotry of the old world in the general societal dislike of Catholicism. Slavery was in effect, Charleston as the foremost American port of that practice. There was a dearth of funding and resources, so much so that he traveled back to Europe three times to raise funds and recruit personnel assistance in the form of sisters and priests. Travel was a most difficult challenge.

Monsignor O'Brien had similar impairment as a newly ordained priest from Pennsylvania moving to the South where there remained a vestige of post-Civil War animosity. In short order, he faced a world war, an influenza pandemic, the age of prohibition, and the Great Depression. In all of this chaos, he remained vigilant of purpose to establish the high school. He raised funds – with the help of Father May – when there was very little to be donated. His vision of a Catholic co-educational high school may have been a 'tough sale' during difficult times. He saw young men that he taught enter a Second World War, comforting families when some did not return. The deficiencies never dissuaded him from his pastoral duties. He performed as if divine providence had guided him to each stage.

Though the world presented itself to be constant in its internal strife, whether it had been penal codes, extreme bias, two World Wars, or economic depression, John England and Joseph Laurence O'Brien lived Christ's message. Their commonality enjoyed was the love for all of God's diverse children. Their adherence to the principle of 'love God, love thy neighbor' can be preened from all that is written and spoken about their disconnected lifetimes. The celebratory evaluation of a hundred year-old high school and two hundred year-old diocese are ostensibly a celebration of these two lives.

There are holy waters to behold – refreshed, renewed, and re-inspired for the centuries that will follow. They have flowed forth and blessed a mighty flock.

CHAPTER TEN

FOUNDATIONS

John England brought a fledgling America to a sense of meaningful progress well beyond his three-state diocese. He built foundations of organization, democratic principles, scholarship and learning, care for humankind, and fundamental separations that are evident two centuries hence. He built essential interreligious trust that scarcely existed before his impact. He established important dialogue and written communication between Catholics, political entities, independent countries, the Vatican, and even his own clergy. He fearlessly stated and reinforced his well-based and articulated principles, though not always popular.

In building a foundation to a high school, the mental image of bricks and mortar give way to the iconic image of the mission it would embrace. After all, several iterations of brick and mortar that were once the high school no longer exist. The foundation mission that Father O'Brien envisioned remains. He wanted to advance Catholic education to a level that heretofore had not existed in the Holy City of Charleston. He did so without wavering. In doing so, he continued the vision of the first prelate, John England. The foundation of developing young people – male and female – in the enrichment of faith, physical endeavor, and educational prowess remains.

Foundations can wash away should they not be anchored deep and wide; should they not be constructed of unfailing material. To the edification of future generations, the foundations set forth by Bishop John

England and Monsignor Joseph Laurence O'Brien meet the Builder's specifications. Real foundations are made of trust.

Catholicism has flourished in the See of the Diocese, Charleston. Initially, England found the three states with less than 1% Catholic population. The Holy City and its metropolitan area have more Catholics than the other large metro areas of the state, now at 8%. Other large metropolitan cities in the original diocese have grown, as well. Charlotte has 9.7%, Savannah 8.5%, Atlanta 16% and Raleigh 6%.[97] The Catholic Church continues to grow in the American South, but that region has been historically the least populated by the papists.

It is interesting to ponder the words of Bishop Francis Kenrick of Philadelphia on the subject of John England being under-utilized upon in his role in Charleston.

> *(The) Charleston diocese is not a fit theatre for a man of his splendid talents... and I would at any moment resign my mitre to make place for him. This I authorize you to communicate to the Sacred Congress.... I had proposed him for the administration of New York, which most sadly needs an efficient Prelate..."*[98]

It may have been that England was in the right place, after all. The South was in need of strong leadership and found in England a man unafraid of speaking his mind, but most willing to show respect for all factions. His foundation of trust and service became a model for the bishops that followed, and especially for the monsignor, Joseph Laurence O'Brien to emulate. Their foundation of faith remains through organization, education, and their subsequent orchestration of both.

CHAPTER ELEVEN

A MAN FOR ALL TIMES

It may be that there can only be one person of an age that defines his time such as John England from the late eighteenth to mid-nineteenth centuries. He administered to his constituency, the Catholic Church and its flock, most graciously. He went beyond to build a lasting legacy that has inspired numerous volumes of great books in the years well past his lifetime. The aspects of the man are as countless color shades upon a prism. And like a prism, the sight of the richness of hue mesmerizes the onlooker with each dancing ray of sunlight. There will be those reading about John England with profound fascination into the coming centuries.

The process of beatification and canonization to sainthood is the distinct course of action reserved to the Pontiff. This is a most diligent procedure that inspects the lives of very holy men and women across the Catholic Faith. There is but one proper manner which canonization can be proposed and accomplished. However, there is at least one source of public discourse that suggests the beatification and sainthood of Bishop John England. Authors Leonard Swidler and Ingrid Shafer of the Association for the Rights of Catholics in the Church (ARCC) advocate the inspection of the lives of both Archbishop John Carroll and Bishop John England as potential American saints.[99]

The authors assemble impressive argument supporting the cause for beatification. In doing so, they inspect Bishop England's contemporary prelates to include those opposed to some of his visionary changes. They cite the personal relationship and appreciation he had gained from Pope Gregory XVI. They relate the admiration of others to include President Andrew Jackson and Secretary of State Martin Van Buren. They point to the bishop's two-continent accomplishments, as well as his proposals of changes that occurred after his lifetime – changes he authored with a futuristic disposition.

Notably, he thrived in a diocese that was 99% non-Catholic, and earned lasting friendships well beyond those that shared his Catholic faith. He advocated national councils for bishops, which were granted in his lifetime and continue today. They were not immediately embraced. He preached in churches of other denominations to perform the Catholic Mass, thankful for the beneficence of other religious leaders whom allowed the use. He preached before the South Carolina State Legislature frequently, by invitation. His adherence to austerity and poverty built admiration and trust in a community of considerable affluence. He was not a man of insular stances when others advocated such. He supported democracy as an intrinsic value to be invested both secularly and inside the institutions of faith. His masterful use of language and inflection were indicators of a brilliant mind brilliantly utilized. His death was mourned locally, nationally, and internationally.

One reference to Father Baker, the Chaplain of the Washington Light Infantry at the time of England's passing eloquently summarizes his impact amongst his diocese as well as his country and community:

> *"That it is with no ordinary feelings of sorrow that the company this publicly recognizes the loss from among its members of the Right Reverend Bishop England. The eloquent tones that have stirred our hearts as with the sound of a trumpet shall no more command and arrest our attention. The lips ever devoted to the advancements of virtue and religion are forever mute, frozen into silence by the icy hand of death. The earnest vindicator of the liberty of his native land, the devoted admirer and constant advocate of the institutions of this, his adopted country; the man of unimpeached and*

unimpeachable character, of intellect and acquirements wide and far-reaching, of imagination fervid and poetic—the priest of self-denying and self-sacrificing virtues, whom all men of every sect and faith delight to honor—the careful and sleepless watcher over the flock committed to his care—has finished his earthly course."[100]

Though his life's work and forward vision may continue to be scrutinized and estimated for its significance, there might never come a day when the papacy may elevate this humble man to the level of saintly consideration. It is for those who study and evaluate his 'life and times' today to ascertain a relevance to our own lives. Where would the Catholic Church in America be had John England never arrived at our harbor? Where would the struggles of his native Ireland be without his brave writings? Where would the discourse of interreligious communication and tolerance have diverted? Bishop John England truly changed his times and the times hence.

Inside the dome of St. Peter's Basilica at The Vatican.   Photo by Author.

CHAPTER TWELVE

THE NAMESAKE HIGH SCHOOL IN ITS FIRST HUNDRED YEARS

The high school that bears the name of the great bishop and established by the great monsignor is now at a celebratory age. There are decades of growth nurtured by clergy and laity alike. Indeed, the first lay principal of the high school made a remarkable impact. Nicholas J. Theos operated the high school as a business from 1973 to 1998, its last year on Calhoun Street. Other capable principals, David Held and Michael Bolchoz have followed. Patrick Finneran leads the high school into its second century.

Father O'Brien had a concise vision for the high school project. Of note were the three short tenets found in the private papers of the O'Brien family tendered to the Diocesan Archives in 2014.

> *"We want to build a high school whose students will excel academically, physically, and spiritually,"* he wrote in a letter to Bishop Henry P. Northrop in November of 1914.[101]

Timing was right and the enthusiasm of the Catholic community prevailed. The standing, a full century later, of Bishop England High School reflects encouraging results.

Their annual SAT scores merit amongst the highest in the State of South Carolina each and every year. Their wide academic mission has grown into a college preparation curriculum with most students extending their education well beyond the 12ᵗʰ grade. Their website shows that over the current seven-year graduation statistics, they had produced a 98% rate of progression of its students into higher education. Students from Bishop England High School usually fare very well at higher levels of education. The high school has also boasted multiple generations of students from many local families, in addition to the infusion of other like-minded families newer to the Charleston area. It has become a popular private alternative to the public school system, even for non-Catholics. Student population has generally ranged from 650 to 800 students, though the new 40-acre campus on Daniel Island can expand to house as many as 1100 students. It had been built in anticipation of that eventual growth. It remains a popular academic challenge to students that seek a proper foundation for degrees beyond high school.

The physical mission can likely be interpolated into the performance of the school's many athletic teams spanning the past century. Though 'Doc' O'Brien was an avid basketball fan and oversaw the plans for the school's first basketball gymnasium shortly before his 1947 retirement as Rector, he could not have imagined the lofty degree of its athletic prowess. Bishop England High School athletic teams have won well in excess of 100 state championships – touching every sport, male and female – in that time. They have won more state championships than any other South Carolina high school. An article in *Sports Illustrated*, written in 2005, rated Bishop England High School as the pre-eminent sports high school in the State of South Carolina and among the best in the country.[102] Another 2013 article in *USA Today* placed the Battling Bishops as among the Top Ten national athletic high school programs.[103]

As to the most important mission of spirituality, again there has been heralded success. Not only has the high school graduated many that have dedicated their lives to religious orders and sought other higher religious plateaus in their personal lives, but the aspect of teaching the subject of religion in a focused four-year program has vaulted the school to become the largest non-secular high school in the state. Religion, as many have described, is the major reason that parents send their children to Bishop England High School. Each day is started and ended by prayer, a decided counter to the prevailing secular restrictions imposed on public education.

The Principal serving the school for the Centennial Anniversary, Mr. Patrick Finneran, reinforces the visionary aspects of Father O'Brien:

> "The high school is dedicated to the very same principles from that initial year of 1915. We advocate a well-rounded education that includes Father O'Brien's guidelines of educational enlightenment, physical development, and spiritual growth. Now, the school appeals to others outside of the Catholic Religion. Nearly 25% of our students are non-Catholic. But they are equally afforded the same value system we encourage for all. We teach much more than academic lessons here. We even have a program for those with other hardships, and they are able to thrive within the environment we administer with great care. It is an attribute to the founders, the alumni and parents, as well as our current faculty that Bishop England High School prepares for the new challenges of its second century."

Ostensibly, Father O'Brien envisioned a need for the development of young people in these three key areas of mind, body, and soul. One hundred years later, a century-of-progress reflects results of which he would be justly proud.

Bishop England High School graduates Joseph P. Riley, Jr. '60, Michael Robinson '61, and Michael Duffy '61 with St. Patrick's Day Grand Marshall, Charleston Bishop Robert Guglielmone. Photo by Author.

Chapter Thirteen

THE CALL

Building a consensus for a need is often an arduous process. In the study of the two Irish lineage priests that have built foundations of Catholicity and Judeo-Christian brotherhood in Charleston, it became apparent that they thrived at this process. The calling to religious orders has been on decline for several decades. Young gentlemen and young ladies have not been entering religious service in the healthy numbers generated in the past. The calling is both worthy and difficult. Parishes across the United States have either closed or consolidated with others. Catholic Hospitals have seen a profound reduction of religious orders dedicated to the sick. Lay teachers have replaced clergy nearly universally. Seminarians are scant; novices are in startlingly regressive numbers. The call is not being heard as it once was.

Perhaps that trend will reverse beyond our lifetimes. There are certainly lives that have been studied, like John England and Joseph Laurence O'Brien, who have inspired many others. O'Brien himself was inspired by England. Understanding their impact upon the world gives testimony to their respective life's work. They each set standards. Their example alone will be studied well past contemporary times and others will be stirred to follow. The advent of digital information broadens the scope of their lives long past quills and inkwells.

The beloved priests and sisters have already followed.

For instance, a third 'Irish-lineage priest' could be meritoriously added to the specter of greatness ascribed to the modern Bishop England

High School. Reverend Monsignor Robert J. Kelly (1927–2004), of Hartford, Connecticut, served as Rector of Bishop England High School from 1964 to 1990. The young Kelly played professional baseball in the Boston Braves organization from 1945 to 1952. Among his teammate friends was the greatest of the Harlem Globetrotters, Meadowlark Lemon, who played in an inconceivable streak of 9925 winning basketball games.[104] Lifelong friends, Lemon visited Father Kelly on occasion at the 203 Calhoun Street campus. Personally humble, Father Kelly's sports abilities sealed many friendships in other communities before arriving in Charleston. But it was in Charleston that he was cherished.

Father Robert J. Kelly
His athleticism and love of sports was emulated by many students.
Photo courtesy Bishop England High School.

Father Kelly was ordained in 1953. His exceptional athletic talent was often demonstrated on the baseball diamond, tennis courts, and in the aptly named Father O'Brien Gymnasium where he played pickup games with the students and the faculty. Often seen carrying *The*

Sporting News, Father Kelly built a legacy of athletic enthusiasm at Bishop England High School. A stern disciplinarian, the Rector gained great affection from a generation of students. He assisted in the physical transition of the high school to Daniel Island in 1998. His religious attributes were always ingrained within his warmth of character. Though there exist records of Baptisms and especially the sacrament of Holy Matrimony, the impressive demand of his officiate services by former students bears mention. He had the ability to be close to his flock, much like 'Doc' O'Brien, to the point that his influence was both deep and wide.

His passing in 2004 did leave another legacy, and an iconic sculptured bronze bench posturing his image in the courtyard of the new school he visited often – especially during athletic contests. The baseball field is named for him. Father Kelly often brought out the best in his students, usually building long-term friendships that transcended the four years of growth the school inured. Quite the competitor, many a fine athlete in the 1960's and 1970's marveled at his considerable skills, abilities of mentorship, and example of sportsmanship.

The sisters have served the community in nearly every aspect, as well. The students knew them by the first names of Saints whom they emulated, never really learning their last names. They taught, healed, prayed, and inspired. They were in evidence at our parochial schools, hospitals, and, of course, Bishop England High School. They were unassuming, yet essential personalities that advanced the grasp of the student's world ahead. They were unforgettable religious women with an abundance of preparation and energy for the challenge – such as Sister Margaretta, Sister Amelia, Sister Miriam, Sister Ann Francis, Sister Marie, Sister Mary Joseph and Sister Mary Louise. There are so many more who have formed little fingers around pencils, taught the Catechism, and brought the world to young minds through literature.

Where will Catholicity turn in the need for pastoral care? In the United States, the last fifty years show a startling reduction in seminarians – from 8,335 in 1965 to 3,631 in 2014.[105] In that same period, the U.S. has shown a significant drop in priests from 58,632 to 38,275. Yet, the worldwide population of priests has remained relatively static.

Thus, there are more priests emigrating from other countries to fill the void of U.S.-born priests. The Catholic population has doubled in that same fifty-year period. There are nearly 1.25 billion Catholics world-wide, 75 million in the United States. Catholics represent 24% of the U.S. population.[106] There remains a pronounced dearth of young women in service to the Church, as well. There were 179,954 sisters serving parishes, schools, hospitals, orphanages, and communities in 1965. A Georgetown University study reports only 49,883 in 2014.[107] But unlike the priesthood, the last fifty years shows nearly a 30% decline in the population of religious sisters.

Ostensibly, the responsibility falls upon the Catholic family. Lay service to the Catholic Church must continue to support the needs of the Catholic Community – as well as Catholic Charities that serve others well outside of the Catholic sphere. These are seen today in the form of deacons, Eucharistic Ministers, lay teachers, retired nurses and doctors that assist outreach missions – and a plethora of other needs fulfilled by volunteers. That need remains profound.

In an ever-changing world, the call to assist or support by the assets of time, talent, and treasure have become even more important. It is within the selfless legacy of John England, who walked the streets of Charleston with worn-out and missing shoe soles, that the quiet act of self-sacrifice becomes part of the Catholic psyche. It is from the humble principles of Joseph Laurence O'Brien that we strive to elevate our next generation to the promise of learning and the fulfillment of greater understanding.

Bishop John England authored a prayer that is repeated daily by the order he founded, the Sisters of Charity of Our Lady of Mercy. With this prayer, we conclude.

PRAYER OF BISHOP JOHN ENGLAND

Blessed Jesus,
I devote and consecrate myself this day
To your honor and service.
In whatsoever way
It shall please You to dispose of me.
Direct my superiors to point out that path
Whither You wish me to go,
And give me the grace to obey.
Holy Virgin, Mother of my Savior,
I place myself
Under your special patronage,
Obtain for me from your Son
All the graces
Which my weakness stands in need of.
Protect me in life and
Defend me in death.
Amen.

Chapter Fourteen

THE PILGRIMAGE
TO THE PATH

O n a personal note, it was after the 2014 book published on the two priests—England and O'Brien—that a sense of incompletion set in. It was not because of the brevity, but rather because of the one-world view. The question beckoned, "What was it like in John England's Cork?" As someone who had traveled there previously, yet without that express question postured, going there again was a compelling senti-ment. I decided I had to go back to find the beginnings of the historical religious hero who had fully captured my interest.

Owing to this itinerary and subsequent recording of the impres-sions, it will be necessary to transition to the first person from the third. Indeed, it was both a spiritual and personal experience of consequence.

The "pilgrimage" was chronicled the by recording daily notes. In mid-September of 2015, a tenth trip to Ireland was in order. Indeed, the journey was more of a pilgrimage than a voyage. There was a definitive sense of journalistic purpose in the pursuit.

With reverent acknowledgement, my 1970 Bishop England High School classmate and good friend, Rev. Anthony Thompson, had lost his wife, Myra, in the egregiously horrid Mother Emmanuel Church murders of June 17, 2015. Along with other Bishop England High School 1970 classmates, we established a memorial garden (Myra's Garden) in the rear of his pastored church, Holy Trinity Reformed Episcopal Church, at 51 Bull Street.

Just three months removed from the tragedy, it was difficult not to think of Anthony Thompson and his family throughout this trip. It was good to be in churches along the way. Prayers were offered to assist his family in the aftermath. He has been a true friend and his loss is profoundly shared.

It was a calling that had me traveling to Cork, eyes wide open, seeking "the way of a holy man," Bishop John England. He was there from 1786 to 1820. The U.S. was a fledgling new country then. He studied our new way of life as we enjoyed it—free citizens in the land of the free. It was not a condition that existed in John England's Ireland.

The journal was created for that idea of posterity. It is posterity that records now for the future about the past. That busy week revealed the purposeful focus upon the senses that one might capture well beyond the printed word. It was a hectic travel schedule that was self-inflicted beyond reason. I should explain the other details before anyone lights candles or begins a Novena.

After several scheduled public events related to my fulfillment of volunteerism activities in Charleston, I packed lightly for a whirlwind adventure. Even my wife figured that I was a bit overly optimistic in my scheduling. The attraction of Ireland was pulling like the sense that the moon pulls the tides to the inlets of my hometown.

My first stop was Greensboro, North Carolina, to meet with the Commissioner of the Atlantic Coast Conference, John Swofford, to discuss a potential NCAA football bowl game for Charleston. His older brother, Oliver Swofford, had a hit song in the 1960s, "Good Morning Starshine." From Greensboro I flew to Boston by an invitation of the Medal of Honor Society to give a report at their annual convention. After that meeting, I was off to Logan International Airport and to Ireland on an overnight transport via Ryanair. Boston to Shannon, Ireland, is only a six-hour flight.

Addressing the National Medal of Honor Convention
on Thursday Morning in Boston

After landing early on Friday morning, I drove to Cork in rain (naturally) to meet some friends expecting my arrival. They had done much to accommodate my research. The first edition publication of this book, *Holy Waters of Charleston*, was enhanced by Eamonn and Karen Cassidy. Eamonn, to me, *is* the Irish Chamber of Commerce. And Karen is the historical research champion in Ireland I could not have imagined.

Eamonn and Karen Cassidy of Cork, Ireland.
Photo courtesy Karen Cassidy.

With the notes and periodic photo documentation of the sites related to the early years of John England I felt that I could compile key information. I anticipated photos of Bandon, Carlow, Cork City, and St. Finbarr's Church (where I planned to attend Sunday Mass). But I was also hoping to find what the French would call the "lagniappe"—something extra that would be unanticipated.

John England did not have the option of a six-hour flight. He boarded a ship at Queenstown (now Cobh) and landed in Charleston more than two months later. Four Irish sisters and another Catholic priest accompanied him, as did his younger sister, Joanna.

Travel in 1820 across oceans was long and tedious.
Photo courtesy Library of Congress.

The 34-year old John England was consecrated as bishop at St. Finbarr's Church in 1820. Note that the good Saint Finbarr has two r's in Ireland, but just one r in the church Bishop England began in Charleston. In Cork City, St. Finbarr's is the correct name, but it is not what the locals call that 1766 church. There, it is the South Chapel. It's confusing because the North Presentation Chapel is actually the Cathedral of St Mary and St. Anne. Also, there is an Anglican cathedral of St. Finbar in Cork.

The North Presentation Convent (still a convent) near the Cathedral of St. Mary & St. Ann's in Cork. It is home to 120 sisters.

In Cork, a Holy Order of Sisters was founded in 1775, though the name was established in 1791.[108] The Sisters of the Presentation of the Blessed Virgin Mary have a convent that still houses one hundred and twenty sisters immersed in the works of charity and education.

Being unaware of the Irish event calendar for the fall, fortuitous timing ensued. The 100th anniversary of the opening of Bishop England High School in Charleston, would occur while on the pilgrimage. There were other Irish anniversaries.

After arrival at Shannon Airport near 7 a.m., I drove to Cork. I did so foregoing the sleep tendency to the excitement of driving on the wrong side of the road while on the wrong side of the rental car. No person or animal was injured in the making of this decision. Along the way, I had hoped those Irish drivers would recognize a lost Charlestonian and allow room for error. It was my intention to keep the fenders of the rental car intact.

Driving on the wrong side is fun once you get used to it.

To stay awake I listened to the Irish news broadcast. The broadcast reminded me of my propitious timing. Since I had already scheduled this trip to coincide with the 100-year anniversary of the opening of Bishop John England's namesake high school (September 22, 1915), other anniversaries were a bonus. The ceremony announced on the radio for a later live television broadcast was quite historical. The remains of the Irish Patriot Thomas Kent were disinterred from Dublin and brought to Cork on the 99th year anniversary of his execution. The event remains a blight upon British-Irish history. It was a national day of observation in Ireland.

Thomas Kent, the fourth of nine Kent children from Cork, was an Irish national hero. He was executed as part of the Easter Rebellion of 1916, though he was not in Dublin for this tragic event. He was made an example in a crackdown after the rebellion. Songs are written about Kent, who was a sports star and had lived for a time in Boston. Here I was, another Thomas, the fourth of nine, coming on a plane from Boston when the whole of Ireland, the President, the Taoiseach, etc., were focused upon Kent's disinterment and saluted reburial as an Irish patriot. The solemn reburial event took place in his hometown just twenty minutes from my hotel. Since no commoner like myself could get close to the dignitaries and ceremony, I watched the entire event via Irish television upon my arrival at the hotel. The ceremony included a formal Mass of Christian burial and the eulogy was given by Mr. Enda Kenny, Ireland's Taoiseach (similar to Prime Minister). The Irish, especially those around Cork City, consider Thomas Kent to be a major catalyst for their independence movement. Irish independence was granted just seven years after his execution. The main train station in Cork is "Kent Station."

Coincidentally, and related to the centuries-old conflict, Bishop John England was quite controversial in Cork. It was because he bravely stood up to the ruling faction, the British, in opposition to their ability to veto Catholic clergy. He must have had mixed emotions about leaving his large family (9 siblings) to start again in a faraway country. He had been an advocate of the American template for independence. He wished such independence for Ireland, no doubt. His consecration date? September 21, 1820! So I will be there to represent our beloved Charleston. I had pre-arranged a meeting with the parish priest there, Father Kerry Murphy-O'Connor.

The statuary is whimsical at nearby Fota Island.
Photo by author.

Cork City is old, young, and spirited. A walk through the downtown area reveals the stonework of yesteryear near the exhilaration of today. There are art galleries, museums, and theaters interspersed in a youthful culture of commerce and entertainment. It is clean and fresh, yet scarred and nostalgic. There are broad walking areas and quaint alleyways leading down to the River Lee. Like Charleston, the profile is low, and the church steeples dominate the gray-blue sky. It is a college town. UCC is University College Cork. That domination of education has spurred the economy with a youthful injection of walkers, browsers, and shoppers.

Though the city spreads out to areas named Midleton, Youghal (pronounced "Ya'll"), Carrigaline, and Ballincollig, the full metro population is less than 400,000.[109] The Charleston metropolitan area approaches 800,000 in 2020.[110]

Eamonn Cassidy & Father Kerry Murphy-O'Connor at
St. Patrick's Church, Bandon.
A copy of the 2014 Edition of "Holy Waters of Charleston" was gifted.

Saturday's busy schedule had me excited about finding the lost parish ruins at Bandon and the warning sentiment of the town ("Turk, Jew and Atheist May Enter, but no Papist"). John England's parish church in Bandon had been difficult to locate. It was necessary to recruit local assistance. The parish church no longer existed, but the perimeter area of town, Kilbrogan, where it once was still had the ruins.

It was my good fortune to have friends in Cork—Eamonn and Karen Cassidy who are experts on Cork history and know much about John England. Bishop England was a major voice in Cork and in all of Ireland before his departure. The students at our namesake high school would be quite proud to mention that name in Cork.

A miserable rain had set in on Sunday. I had lunch with my Cork friends after the Sunday Mass. Because of my unfamiliarity with the Irish roads around Cork, Ireland's second largest city, I gladly accepted the suggestion that my friend Eamonn would drive to places of interest.

September 21st is the passing of the summer into the fall but has significance more than that on this pilgrimage-walk through Cork and surroundings. Surely it was on a Monday that, a century ago, Father J. L. 'Doc' O'Brien opened rented space that would become Bishop John England Memorial High School. An academic, he must have known the Cork history of Bishop John England. I have walked those steps purposefully to imagine the times and the consequences.

St. Patrick's College is located in Carlow, Ireland
Photo Courtesy of St. Patrick's College.

It was on September 21st in 1690 that the walled City of Cork was besieged by the forces of William of Orange, commanded by John Churchill. Yes, it's that same Churchill family we can trace back through Sir Winston. It was on September 21st of 1820 that Fr. John England was consecrated as Bishop of Charleston in St. Finbarr's Church (called the *North Chapel* then). He then sailed to Charleston to arrive on the last Sunday of 1820. There is no doubt that he left as an appeasement to the ruling British. He had been an outspoken opponent to the *Veto* that allowed the British to approve church appointments. In addition, he would not swear allegiance to the British Crown—a slight that could escalate to a death warrant. A contemporary of the *Irish Liberator*, Daniel O'Connell, he was similarly a constant challenger to the precepts of British rule. Both O'Connell and England attended college contemporaneously in Carlow. They were friends who became ardent cross-supporters. England's consecration and subsequent deportation may have been quite suitable to the authorities.

John England was born on September 23, 1786, and managed several interesting anecdotes to be found here. He was the first priest ordained in the then-new Cathedral of St. Mary's and St. Anne's. It opened in August of 1808. I visited the Cathedral, as well. He was ordained on October 10th of 1808. He was the only Catholic student in the Green Coat School—and apparently this experience was helpful in his ability to find common ground with the Anglicans there. The former Green Coat School was located—but is now a retail establishment. I found other pertinent history of the first Charleston Bishop in Cork. He was the first teacher and first president of St. Mary's Seminary, opened on September 13, 1813. September seems to be a "happening" month in so many aspects here.

A view of the River Lee in Cork City Center.
I took this photo from the south side, looking north. Idyllic!

A 1950's renovation of the Cathedral of St. Mary and St. Anne inte-rior ruined its Gothic character. The regretful renovation was the opin-ion of the priest, Father Ted Sheehan. That said—I fully agree. Father Sheehan gave me a tour, to include a basement visit and history display that had much on John England.

*A display board on John England at the Cathedral of St. Mary
and St. Anne. I took this photo in the basement of the Cathedral,
thanks to the assistance of Father Ted Sheehan.*

In visiting the significant sites of the Corkman John England, it should be noted that the hills rolling down to the River Lee in the city are mindful of those in San Francisco, though not as steep. Much of his daily activities were performed in a parish setting not much more than a mile squared. The main commercial occupation in the immediate area was a butter factory, where butter was shipped throughout much of Europe and to America. Wherever there were British troops, butter was packaged with high salt content (as a preservative).

England's childhood home is unknown, but it would be much like the tenements still existing in the parish. The roads are hilly and serpentine and the narrow alleys may have been the play yard for many large Catholic families. The straighter roads were part of a grid system developed years later.

Tenements near St. Finbarr's Church.
Signage revealed that the first Irish immigrant was from here.

His parish church (St. Finbarr's) is the oldest Catholic Church still standing in Cork (1766). I returned and attended Mass there as planned. There have been some additions and renovations inside, but the church remains much the same as it did in 1808 when John England tended that flock—along with the nuns at the North Presentation Chapel around the corner (nearer to the Cathedral).

While at the St. Finbarr church, I was able to obtain a certificate of baptism for John England (September 25, 1786), which I later delivered to Bishop England High School. Note that his baptism was at the Cathedral. Yet his consecration as Bishop of Charleston was at the church of his youth, St. Finbarr's.

Parish of _St Mary & St Anne_ Diocese of _Cork & Ross_

On examination of the Register of Baptisms of the above parish

I certify that according to it _John England_

was born on the _____ day of _____

and was baptised according to the Rites of the Catholic Church

on the _25th_ day of _Sept 1786_

in the Church of _St Mary & St Anne_

by the Rev _Fr C Horgan_

Parents _Thomas England & Honora Lordan_

Sponsors _John Walsh & Catherine Moylan_

Confirmed _____

Married _____

Given on the _19th_ day of _Sept 215_

Signed Rev _Bernard Mullane_

BIRTH AND
BAPTISMAL
CERTIFICATE

St Mary & St Anne
North Cathedral
Roman Street
Cork

L.S.

Known also
as the
"North Chapel"

VERITAS

I also visited St. Anne's Church near this area, where one can climb the stairs and ring the bells. It is the oldest continuous-use church in Cork—and is Anglican. I served as a bell-ringer (ringing out the notes to *Amazing Grace*). They have the numbered tunes in a book next to the ropes. (The historic trivia about *Amazing Grace* that the Charleston tour guides tell: The song came from a slave ship captain who escaped a hurricane on his way to Charleston. The captain, John Newton, changed careers and became a clergyman. He jotted the inspiring words inside the Circular Congregational Church in Charleston!)

The square bell tower is called the "Four Faced Liar." That moniker refers to the inaccurate clocks on each side that are not synchronized—each showing the time minutes off from the next.

St. Finbar Cathedral is on the south side of the River Lee. It is an impressive structure, as well. It is Anglican.

The North Chapel... or St. Finbarr's Church, Cork City.
Photo by author.

Finding John England's church in Bandon (29k away) was much more difficult. Fortunately, a visiting priest at St. Patrick's Church was there for a renewal of wedding vows, the aforementioned Fr. Kerry Murphy-O'Connor. I had spoken to him by phone on Friday. It was an unplanned circumstance. He knew where the ruins sat near the edge of town. They are quite difficult to locate unless you know the road-ways of Bandon. It is a wooded area with much over-growth and scant maintenance. Bandon Church is known as the Catholic Church at Kilbrogan—though no church remains, only sacred ruins on a hill. The hill has a rather morbid name, "Gallows Hill." It is properly named by its former use.

Fr. John England was most un-welcome in Bandon, a Protestant stronghold that protected Cork from the west since the late 1500's. An eighteenth-century adage repeated to me was, "Who held that bridge, held Cork." John England entered the West Gates there that had the famed (aforementioned) inscription—"Turk, Jew or Atheist May Enter Here, But No Papist." The sign no longer exists, according to Father Murphy-O'Connor. However, I found from the local Mr. O'Sullivan that an enterprising Catholic added to the sign a witty line before its demise. It read, "Whoever Wrote This Wrote it Well, for the Same is Written on the Gates of Hell." Humor always wins out.

There were more than two thousand gravestones at the newer St. Patrick's Church in Bandon. I didn't count them. Mr. O'Sullivan was the graveyard custodian. There were other crowded graves at the ruins—simply referred to as the Catholic Church Graveyard at Kilbrogan. Apparently, Fr. England was very successful! Catholics came, they lived, they died. There were plenty in Bandon.

Mr. O'Sullivan's conjecture was that the Protestant domination of Bandon is nearly gone. He said that they seemed to drift away or had all daughters, causing the traditional Protestant names to disappear. He noted that, in general, the use of the 'O' denoted a family that "would not take the soup." I had never heard that before. Two centuries prior, starving Irish families could be fed soup if they switched to the Anglican faith. Interesting. Though this is not a universal convention, it speaks volumes about the Irish determination.

Another Bandon saying, O'Sullivan repeated, was that "Pigs were protestant, and ducks wore boots." I don't know what that means, either. But it made him laugh.

The ruins at Fr. John England's church near Kilbrogan (simply an area of Bandon) if you're going—are like something out of a Jane Austen novel. There are stones denoting the lives lost from firing squads, some even with carvings of "God Save Ireland." I took nearly 250 photos in four days, to include some of these sad gravestones. The church ruins would be easy to miss. I noted that some are being currently maintained by families of the deceased and there were several containers of holy water from the Marian Shrine at Lourdes I recognized. The Lourdes bottle container is unmistakable as I have a few myself!

Kilbrogan Catholic Church, Bandon. It was abandoned in 1923. Photo by Author.

The holy water fonts are still in the wall. The grassy road up to the church is behind a heavy iron gate. The graveyard is crowded. I suspect that nearly all plots were used.

By the way, Mr. O'Sullivan stated that he had just turned 73 and that he is the last of the Bandon family of O'Sullivans. Why? He had no brothers - and five daughters! He said that whatever the Protestants succumbed to had eventually infected the Catholics, as well!

As I found living history in Cork, I also found dying history in the gravestones. There is no doubt that the plight of the Irish was substantial with plague, famine, and domination. Yet their religion was vital in uniting the country through it all.

In a way, this wave of doom persists. It was most recently seen as the country adhered to the crest of the Celtic Tiger prior to the economic disasters that impacted the entire world. As my friends from Ireland noted, "We lost 150,000 Euro—but we say it quickly so that it doesn't hurt as much." It is their plight to rise above it, mostly in faith. Then the year 2020 brought on the Coronavirus Covid-19. The Irish prepare for the worst to bring out their best.

The gravestones say as much.

More than 2000 graves cover the hill behind St. Patrick's Church in Bandon.
Photo by author.

We saw a bit of every tribute—from ornamental monuments to a hammered tin scripted and placed in with two loose bricks. There were all-too-many tributes to the fallen who had been killed in their freedom fight or executed for the cause of an independent Ireland.

I asked about one of the prominent monuments at Bandon that was marked "IRB." That stood for the Irish Republican Brotherhood, precursor to what we know as the "IRA." I noted that a young man was executed. The stone in the graveyard mentioned the death of the entombed "at the hands of the Saxon," in what was chiseled as a derisive message by a family in grief.

"…At the Hand of the Saxons…"
Photo by author.

A previous St. Michael's Church (Kilbrogan) at this site was built in 1796 but burned down by the Scottish in 1798 related to the major uprising that year. Previously, as insult, the stones were used to build the Holy Trinity Protestant Church in Bandon.

This "Catholic Church Kilbrogan" was again rebuilt (around 1804) prior to Father John England's 1817 arrival. Finally, due to a failed roof and poor financial support, it became the "Abandoned church at Bandon (1923)." The setting was peaceful and away from the sounds of traffic.

Sad Note on the Times...
Photo by author.

I copied an interesting part of its history from the Diocesan records at Cork and Ross:

KILBROGAN IN THE LATE NINETEENTH CENTURY

"Most Rev. Dr. Delaney, Bishop of Cork was born in the Sacristy attached to the Church on Christmas day 1804. His father, a weaver by trade, and his mother a member of the Quinlan family, lived just beyond Kilbrogan Street, near the well, which is still known to locals, as the Bishops Well.

Bishop Delaney was ordained at the age of 24 and having spent some time as a curate in Cork city, he was appointed Parish Priest of Bandon in 1845. Two years later as the famine stalked the land; he was made Bishop of Cork and ruled the Diocese for 39 years. He died on the 14th November 1886 and was interred in the Cemetery at the Ursuline Convent, Blackrock, Cork."

So, a future Bishop of Ireland was born in the old Kilbrogan Church sacristy on Christmas Day, 1804! He was likely in the parish of young John England's care when England arrived at the same parish in 1817. It is conjecture, but I wonder if Father John England inspired the youngster Delaney, who would rise to the important role as Bishop?

The Irish pastoral countryside reflects an agrarian culture.
Photo by author.

Having walked that path, it was easy to think of John England and the tasks he had undertaken. He had to be a man of great fortitude.

My return to Charleston was complicated in ticketing through Boston via DC. It had been as suggested—a whirlwind. It took twenty-three hours to get home—a self-inflicted penance for poor scheduling. Pope Francis was to be in Washington, D.C., as I slipped through. He was in Rome when I was there last, but it seems we keep missing each other!

I would be remiss should I not mention some of the expressions overheard while moving around the Irish countryside. They humored me all along the way.

At Fota Island, "He was emboldened like the first man to eat an oyster."

At Cork City, "A lad without freckles is a sky without stars."

Upon learning of an engagement, also in Cork, "A man needs to get married to complete himself; then he's surely finished!"

At Ballybunion, "I was so cash poor back then, I couldn't pay a compliment."

Lastly, at Shannon Airport, "I only find two occasions to drink these days—when I'm thirsty and when I'm not!"

When we tally the end of anything—an adventure, an experience, a moment or a life— we would be remiss not to be humbled by it all and thankful for the friends we made along the way.

Having a coffee at Ballybunion the day before leaving with old friends I met many years ago (l to r) Anthony Bennett, Seamus Finnerty & Kevin Frost. Photo by author.

There has to be a flash weld or a slow simmer that moves us to do something out of the ordinary. In my case it was the introduction of the Irish poet William Butler Yeats. A professor at The Citadel, James Rembert, brought him alive and immersed my soul into late 19th century Ireland. I visited the Yeats grave in Sligo in 1990. It's not far from the Holy Shrine at Knock (which is a must-see). I envisioned being there for the simple interactions, the labor, the despair, and the constancy of cause. I had imagined the wave of freedom as it reached their shores (1922). I had championed the Irish rise. I had embraced the immensity of their common bond—their ultimate triumph over centuries of suppression. I felt their new frontier through another's words—W. B. Yeats.

The Butter Market at the top of the street in Cork.
Photo by author.

Trudging the uphill streets to see a butter market or a high stone wall where young John England gained his bearing brought Cork City of 200 years ago to my senses. The old schools, the convent, and churches are still there. And so are the gravestones. My Irish friends, Eamonn and Karen, were equally inspired by the experience. We found so much that we had not anticipated—hidden church ruins, old letters of correspondence, and the acknowledgement of Bishop John England's significance on a display board in the cathedral basement.

I'm glad I took the time. I could have jogged my way through, eyes forward. Instead I looked left and right and found some amount of meaning to it all. John England was an exceptional man of high character. His 56 years warranted tedious examination and comment. I hope I have brought some of him to others.

St. Anne's Shandon. The four faced liar! Ring the bells if you go.
Photo by author.

The pilgrimage had been completed. As a layman drifting around with a purpose and the idea to discover more than what was known, I will always feel some attachment to John England and Cork City. I did. John England was like molasses on a waffle in Cork. He is still a part of their rich history. School children know of this man. He can be confirmed as one of their legendary citizens—a man who opened both minds and hearts. We can surely claim him in Charleston, but we should salute Cork as the hot furnace that forged this great man. He was sent as propitiously as any ambassador was ever sent to diffuse political drama between countries. John England set Irish history on a path, and then did as much in America. He is a most appropriate example of triumph to young minds imagining their way into the sometimes-cruel world that may await. His unique devotion was enabled by his admirable strength of faith, his communicative skills, and the obvious wealth of his God-given energy.

Sunset at Ballybunion. If you look far enough, you can see America.
Photo by author.

I ended my adventure at Ballybunion in County Kerry where the sun slipped behind the wind into the sea. The gusts brought a typical Irish sideways rain as the darkness crawled through the dunes.

If one were to look at the game of golf as a microcosm for the Irish spirit, then it would be understood that they were, from the beginning, indomitable. You may have some sense of gaining an upper hand at the turn, but they will brace into the wind, persevere, and find a way to claim little victories along the path. And in the end they will still be standing, wet, rumpled, and weary. But it would be within their expectation for earning a meaningful and worthy prize at the conclusion.

Upon returning from the twenty-three-hour flight connections ordeal, I attended my high school class's 45th Reunion (Thursday, September 24th, 2015). I had hoped no one would ask me what I'd been up to—for their sake! I slept well that evening.

AFTERWORD

The study of two righteous priests within the quilt of their times has gained timeless relevance. They have taught us principles that apply whether one is seventeen or seventy. They have welcomed the ordeal in order to facilitate the ideal.

Science continues to seek the mysteries of life, to improve health, and to discover ways in which humankind can exceed age barriers. Everyone wants to live longer. What we have learned from the lives of Bishop England and Monsignor O'Brien is that living a long life should never be the goal. One should seek to live the wide and selfless life.

Unveiling of the Bishop John England statue at the downtown high school in 1950.
Photo by Albert Sottile courtesy of Bishop England High School.

In living selflessly wide, there is an inherent opportunity to better serve mankind. John England and "Doc" O'Brien expanded their spheres to enjoy spiritual significance in all relationships and in all peoples. The broadened life is one that has no fear, no bias, and no perimeter. There is a unique enthusiasm – a passion – in committing oneself to the sincere and humble service of others. Selflessness is, perhaps, the highest estate one may obtain in the comportment of life. It rises above property, gemstones, and the trappings of wealth. There is a biblical quality in living purposely beyond the fruits of abundance and the temptation of self-aggrandizement.

The world we live in promotes the opposite – the inherited attainment of privilege. Within affluence, material things are bestowed, maintained, and admired. Generational families are often torn apart by the reading of a will or the value of an old portrait. They matter not.

Daughters, barely of driving age, want a new sports car; sons demand the latest video game or cellphone. These are false necessities, though the rationalization of such portends otherwise. When earthly things exceed the connection of a meaningful relationship, our societal values become skewered. Yet, we tend to judge privilege and pretension with astigmatic vision. So much that we deem to be essential are simply the deceptive appraisals of reality. Living wide corrects our vision. A world view brings us to a conclusion that we live as part of humanity. The 2020 pandemic certified the corrective discipline. We need each other and we need our faith beyond.

In the study of the two holy priests we discover that their enthusiasm of life was passed on to others. It became infectious. Those who they met and befriended likely gained an equal enthusiasm for them and what they represented. No doubt, many who crossed paths with these selfless and humble men were inspired to 'live wider' within their own lives. It is not enough, as is ascribed herein, to say, "live selflessly, live wide." One must wholeheartedly commit and perform all aspects of this higher aspiration. Spontaneous and anonymous givers are the best illustration of this attitude.

Bishop John England came to Charleston committed to perform, despite the overwhelming risks of poor funding, non-acceptance—and ultimately his declining health. Father Joseph Laurence O'Brien came under another set of impossible circumstances— hesitant bias, two World Wars, interspersed with a long cycle of economic difficulties. Yet both persevered. What they founded is still here in the form of organizational precepts, religious community, and educational institutions. They rose from being important stewards of their times to a much more elevated plateau of being studied as exemplary and significant figures for all times.

It is all the more inspiring that the path they took had so many impediments, yet so many glorious vistas and warming hearths. Indeed, their early kindling of Catholicity can be felt today in every homily, every sacrament, and every fingertip extended into the holy waters of our next blessing.

Current Bishop of Charleston Robert E. Gugliemone
blesses the students of Bishop England High School.
Photo Courtesy Diocese of Charleston.

THE FIRST 200 YEARS: BISHOPS OF CHARLESTON

John England	(1820-1842)
Ignatius A. Reynolds	(1844-1855)
Patrick N. Lynch	(1858-1882)
Henry P. Northrop	(1883-1916)
William T. Russell	(1917-1927)
Emmet M. Walsh	(1927-1949)
John J. Russell	(1950-1958)
Paul J. Hallinan	(1958-1962)
Francis F. Reh	(1962-1964)
Ernest L. Unterkoefler	(1964-1990)
David B. Thompson	(1990-1999)
Robert J. Baker	(1999-2007)
Robert E. Guglielmone	(2009-Present)[111]

ABOUT THE AUTHOR: W. THOMAS MCQUEENEY

W. Thomas McQueeney is a native Charlestonian and has authored eleven books centered upon his beloved city. McQueeney, one of nine children, grew up in the hospital area just blocks from the Ashley River. He graduated from The Citadel as an English major in 1974. The McQueeney family established a record for sibling graduates—six—at the military college. A local businessman, community volunteer, and artist, McQueeney was presented *The Order of the Palmetto* in 2009—the highest designation award for a citizen of South Carolina. He continues his engagement with the community by serving as chairman of The National Medal of Honor Leadership and Education Center. He grew up in St. Patrick's parish and is a member of Christ Our King parish. He is married and has four children.

ATTRIBUTIONS AND ENDNOTES

1 BEHS move to Daniel Island. https://www.behs.com/about/our-story/

2 War of 1812. https://www.biography.com/us-president/andrew-jackson

3 Spanish Flu Misnomer. https://slate.com/technology/2018/10/spanish-flu-1918-influenza-pandemic-name-misnomer.html

4 St. Patrick College, Carlow Ireland. http://www.carlowcollege.ie/Our-College

5 Stations of the Cross. https://www.catholiccompany.com/getfed/how-to-pray-the-stations-of-the-cross/

6 John Locke. Fundamental Constitutions of Carolina. http://johnlocke.org/about/who_is_john_locke_essay.html

7 Fundamental Constitutions of Carolina. https://www.carolana.com/Carolina/Documents/fundamental_constitutions_overview.html

8 Penicillin and Polio vaccines. https://www.historyofvaccines.org/timeline/polio

9 Estimate of Catholics in 1832. http://www.newadvent.org/cathen/05470a.htm

10 Haitian Revolution. https://www.blackpast.org/global-african-history/haitian-revolution-1791-1804/

11 French Revolution. https://www.nationalarchives.gov.uk/education/resources/french-revolution/

12 Irish Uprising 1798. https://www.britannica.com/event/Irish-Rebellion-Irish-history-1798

13 Society of United Irishmen 1798. http://www.bbc.co.uk/history/british/empire_seapower/irish_reb_01.shtml

14 Acceptance of Catholics. http://www.historytoday.com/jonathan-clark/american-revolution-war-religion

15 Simmons, Agatha Aimar. Brief History of St. Mary's Roman Catholic Church. Page 10. Published 1961, JJ Furlong & Co., Charleston.

16 St. Mary's Vestry. Simmons, Agatha Aimar. Brief History of St. Mary's Roman Catholic Church. Page 18. Published 1961, JJ Furlong & Co., Charleston.

17 St. Mary's Vestry. Simmons, Agatha Aimar. Brief History of St. Mary's Roman Catholic Church. Page 18. Published 1961, JJ Furlong & Co., Charleston.

18 Campbell, Sister Anne Francis, OLM, *Bishop England's Sisterhood 1829-1929*, written dissertation 1968. Introduction, Page 3.

19 Trusteeism. O'Brien, Joseph Laurence. Bishop John England: The Apostle to Democracy. 222 pages.

20 Charles Carroll. https://charlescarrollhouse.org/the-carrolls/personal-biography-2

21 Father de Clorivière. Lhttps://books.google.com/books/about/Joseph_Pierre_Picot_de_Limoëlan_de_Clor.html?id=KvRtNwAACAAJ

22 Peaceful Resolution of Vestry. http://www.cyberfaith.com/examining/roots13.html

23 Diary of Bishop John England. The Life and Times of John England, 1786-1842, Volume One, Dr. Peter Guilday. Published 1927, The American Press.

24 Population 1790 and 1820. http://en.wikipedia.org/wiki/Largest_cities_in_the_United_States_by_population_by_decade#1790

25 1820 census. https://www.census.gov/history/www/through_the_decades/index_of_questions/1820_1.html

26 Joanna England. http://www.catholicdoc.org/ac/?p=collections/findingaid&id=147&q=&rootcontentid=9087

27 Repeal of Irish Penal Codes. http://www.newadvent.org/cathen/11611c.htm

28 John England. http://www.corkandross.org/priests.jsp?priestID=397

29 Kelly, Joseph Charleston's Bishop John England and American Slavery.http://muse.jhu.edu/login?auth=0&type=summary&url=/journals/new_hibernia_review/v005/5.4kelly.html

30 Kelly, Joseph. Charleston's Bishop John England and American Slavery. https://muse.jhu.edu/login?auth=0&type=summary&url=/journals/new_hibernia_review/v005/5.4kelly.html

31 Catholic Correspondence. http://www.catholic-doc.org/ac/?p=collections/findingaid&id=147&q=&rootcontentid=9087

32 St. Finbar's Cathedral, Cork. http://www.corkandross.org/priests.jsp?priestID=397

33 Bandon Inscription. http://www.britannica.com/EBchecked/topic/187865/John-England

34 Bandon acceptance. https://www.britannica.com/biography/John-England

35 Irish Irritant to Crown. http://www.newadvent.org/cathen/05470a.htm

36 Daniel O'Connell. http://www.newadvent.org/cathen/11200c.htm

37 Father Thomas England. https://books.google.com/books?id=6GQNAAAAYAAJ&pg=PA198&lpg=PA198&dq=father+thomas+england+of+cork&source=bl&ots=wYfxA50q-C&sig=ACfU3U3isfedSHJf_iYUy57F7up0pbGlAw&hl=en&sa=X&ved=2ahUKEwis1Yq8n9noAhUCZN8KHWFJBWAQ6AEwBnoECAcQLw#v=onepage&q=father%20thomas%20england%20of%20cork&f=false. Page 198.

38 St. Patrick's Church record. http://www.sccatholic.org/african-american-ministry/black-catholic-history

39 Irish Migrations. http://www.ucc.ie/en/emigre/history/

40 Kelly, Joseph. Charleston's Bishop John England and American Slavery. https://muse.jhu.edu/login?auth=0&type=summary&url=/journals/new_hibernia_review/v005/5.4kelly.html

41 Free Black School. The Life and Times of John England, 1786-1842, Volume One, Dr. Peter Guilday

42 Slavery Quotation. The Life and Times of John England, 1786-1842, Volume One, Dr. Peter Guilday, pages 76-77. Published 1927, The American Press.

43 Ibid.

44 Ibid.

45 Southern Literary Messenger. http://gdc.gale.com/archivesunbound/
archives-unbound-the-southern-literary-messenger-literature-of-the-old-south/

46 Nullification Act. http://www.u-s-history.com/pages/h333.html

47 Bishop England's Speech before Congress. One Truth. http://www.ncregister.
com/site/article/the_first_catholic_voice_before_congress/

48 Bishop England's Speech before Congress. Church and State.http://www.ncreg-
ister.com/site/article/the_first_catholic_voice_before_congress/

49 Bishop England's Speech before Congress. http://www.ncregister.com/site/
article/the_first_catholic_voice_before_congress/

50 DeLorme, Rita H. from article: Bishop John England's *Haytian Legation* http://
diosav.org/sites/all/files/archives/9105p05.pdf

51 Guilday, Peter. *The Life and Times of John England.*

52 DeLorme, Rita H. from article: Bishop John England's *Haytian Legation* http://
diosav.org/sites/all/files/archives/9105p05.pdf

53 Sacred Congregation of the Propaganda is an administration of the Vatican responsible for the spread of Catholicism. http://www.newadvent.org/cathen/12456a.
htm

54 Ibid.

55 Funeral of Bishop John England. http://books.google.com/books?id=4nJLAAA
AMAAJ&pg=PA24&lpg=PA24&dq=funeral+of+Bishop+John+england&source
=bl&ots=Gm_nS0MVTe&sig=sGzRqilJtT_Ihr21krXl7ozJemg&hl=en&sa=X&ei=
UHUDVNiCB8aPNo6NgJgN&ved=0CDIQ6AEwAw#v=onepage&q=funeral%20
of%20Bishop%20John%20england&f=false

56 The New Advent. http://www.newadvent.org/cathen/05470a.htm

57 Bishop England's Passing. http://diosav.org/sites/all/files/archives/S8408p03_0.
pdf

58 Bishop John England Press Award. http://www.ncregister.com/site/article/the_first_catholic_voice_before_congress/

59 Democarcy in Church Affairs. O'Brien, Joseph Laurence. Bishop John England: The Apostle to Democracy. 222 pages.

60 Richard Fuller, DD. http://baptisthistoryhomepage.com/fuller.richard.by.bogard.html

61 Appointment of Bishops from Rome. http://www.arcc-catholic-rights.net/HISTORICAL%20BACKGROUND.htm

62 Ibid

63 Conventions of Bishops. http://www.arcc-catholicrights.net/HISTORICAL%20BACKGROUND.htm

64 Constitution of the Diocese of Charleston. http://www.arcc-catholic-rights.net/HISTORICAL%20BACKGROUND.htm

65 Diocese of Scranton, PA. http://www.newadvent.org/cathen/13633a.htm

66 Diocese of Charleston Archival office. http://www.catholic-doc.org/archive1/?p=collections/findingaid&id=130&q=&rootcontentid=57172

67 Education of Father O'Brien. http://www.catholic-doc.org/archive1/?p=collections/findingaid&id=130&q=&rootcontentid=57172

68 Monsignor O'Brien 1934. http://books.google.com/books?id=lr0SAAAAIAAJ&pg=PA337&lpg=PA337&dq=Monsignor+Joseph+L.+O'Brien&source=bl&ots=63lsaiUZFC&sig=Ut31qvdkEEzJrwYP5n0AFMvF3s4&hl=en&sa=X&ei=-nIEVJD2Oc_JgwTq8oIg&ved=0CDoQ6AEwBTgK#v=onepage&q=Monsignor%20Joseph%20L.%20O'Brien&f=false

69 Early life of Father O'Brien. http://www.catholic-doc.org/archive1/?p=collections/findingaid&id=130&q=&rootcontentid=57172

70 American Catholic Who's Who 1945-1946. http://books.google.com/books?id=lr0SAAAAIAAJ&pg=PA337&lpg=PA337&dq=Monsignor+Joseph+L.+O'Brien&source=bl&ots=63lsaiVYKB&sig=GrGmul5XVIhI6f1vZ8jCX9kq76w&hl=en&sa=X&ei=sHYEVIX6JsuPNuGWgpAJ&ved=0CDoQ6AEwBTgK#v=onepage&q=Monsignor%20Joseph%20L.%20O'Brien&f=false

71 Construction and Renovation Projects. http://www.catholic-doc.org/archive1/?p=collections/findingaid&id=130&q=&rootcontentid=57172

72 Charleston Parochial Schools of 1914. Information gathered from the Archives of the Sisters of Charity of Our Lady of Mercy at May Forest.

73 Albert Wheeler Todd. Notable Charleston-based architect designed the building at Hampstead Square circa 1904.

74 O'Brien Family Papers. Letter to Bishop Northrup.

75 Private Papers of Monsignor Joseph Laurence O'Brien, unpublished. Diocesan Office of Archives. Page 41.

76 Monsignor J.L. O'Brien pamphlet.

77 Bourke Cochran. Circular letter from Rev. J.L. O'Brien to Catholic Community. Archival Office of the Diocese of Charleston.

78 Ibid.

79 Bio of William Bourke Cochran (1854-1923). http://bioguide.congress.gov/scripts/biodisplay.pl?index=C000575

80 Motion Pictures evolution to 'Talkies.' http://xroads.virginia.edu/~UG00/3on1/movies/talkies.html

81 Dancing 1917. Passage taken from the notes and letters of Rev. Msgr. Joseph Laurence O'Brien. Times and methods preened from website as follows:

http://news.google.com/newspapers?nid=1144&dat=19170910&id=s0UbAAAAIBAJ&sjid=aUkEAAAAIBAJ&pg=2346,3160934

82 Circular Letter copy from Rev. J.L. O'Brien. Archives of the Diocese of Charleston.

83 Faculty of Bishop England High School 1916. Archival Office, Diocese of Charleston, Rev. J.L. O'Brien correspondence.

84 Ibid.

85 Dedication to St. Paul. From archival letters and correspondence of the O'Brien family, donated to the Diocese of Charleston in 2014.

86 Father May. https://books.google.com/books?id=TqIzAQAAMAAJ&pg=PA270&lpg=PA270&dq=father+james+j.+may+charleston+sc&source=bl&ots=qWtVAoZG8p&sig=ACfU3U1evx6ECUN75ZYzF87zSdjcyV1ldw&hl=-en&sa=X&ved=2ahUKEwjRr_ud1NnoAhUFZd8KHbgCBUgQ6AEwBHoECAsQKQ#v=onepage&q=father%20james%20j.%20may%20charleston%20sc&f=false

87 Father James J. May. Information from "In Memorium: The Right Reverend Monsignor James J. May 1887-1958.

88 Father James May. Notes from the correspondence of Fr. J.L. O'Brien. Archival Office of the Diocese of Charleston.

89 Ibid.

90 Ibid.

91 Bishop Russell Dedication Speech. Papers of Rev. J.L. O'Brien. Archival Office of the Diocese of Charleston.

92 Curriculum. Correspondence of Rev. J.L. O'Brien. Archival Office. Diocese of Charleston.

93 Ibid.

94 Conference of Christians and Jews. http://books.google.com/books?id=lr0SAAAAIAAJ&pg=PA337&lpg=PA337&dq=Monsignor+Joseph+L.+O'Brien&source=bl&ots=63lsaiVYKB&sig=GrGmul5XVIhI6f1vZ8jCX9kq76w&hl=en&sa=X&ei=sHYEVIX6JsuPNuGWgpAJ&ved=0CDoQ6AEwBTgK#v=onepage&q=Monsignor%20Joseph%20L.%20O'Brien&f=false

95 The Life and Times of John England, 1786-1842, Volume One, Dr. Peter Guilday, pages 76-77. Published 1927, The American Press.

96 Obituary of Father O'Brien's father 1940. http://scr.stparchive.com/Archive/SCR/SCR01281939P21.php

97 Catholic populations in the American South. http://www.ncregister.com/daily-news/catholicism-in-the-south-once-a-strange-religion-now-forging-ahead-with-eva

98 Bishop Kenrick. http://www.arcc-catholic-rights.net/HISTORICAL%20BACKGROUND.htm

99 ARCC advocating of Sainthood. http://www.arcc-catholic-rights.net/HISTORICAL%20BACKGROUND.htm

100 Ibid

101 O'Brien Family Archives of 2014, Donated to the Diocese of Charleston

102 Sports Illustrated. http://www.behs.com/apps/pages/index.jsp?uREC_ID=171694&type=d&termREC_ID=&pREC_ID=352494

103 Top Ten USA Today. www.greatschools.org › South Carolina › Charleston

104 Meadowlark Lemon. http://sports.yahoo.com/nba/news?slug=ycn-11083466

105 Seminarian Population. http://cara.georgetown.edu/caraservices/requested-churchstats.html

106 Catholic Population. http://en.wikipedia.org/wiki/Catholic_Church_by_country

107 Sisters in Service. http://cara.georgetown.edu/caraservices/requestedchurch-stats.html

108 Presentation Sisters. https://www.presentationsisters.org/who-we-are/history/

109 Cork Census 2020. https://worldpopulationreview.com/world-cities/cork-population/

110 Charleston Metro Population 2020. https://worldpopulationreview.com/us-cities/charleston-population/

111 Bishops of Charleston. https://charlestondiocese.org/about/our-history/

Lightning Source UK Ltd.
Milton Keynes UK
UKHW050409050920
369326UK00001B/20